Simply Prepared

A Guide to Emergency Preparedness
and Food Storage

by

Cheryl F. Driggs

CFD Publications
Spring, Texas

Printed in the United States of America.

Cover Design and chapter illustrations by Leo Fortuno, Houston Texas.
Book layout by Cheryl Driggs.

The quote by Ezra Taft Benson on page 8 is from "Prepare Ye" by Ezra Taft Benson from the *Ensign*, January 1974. The quote by Vaughn J. Featherstone on page 25 is from "Food Storage" by Vaughn J. Featherstone from the *Ensign*, May 1976. The quote by Clayton S. Huber on page 29 is from the "Random Sampler" article "Wheat Storage Tip" by Clayton S. Huber from the *Ensign*, October 1980. The quote by John Hal Johnson on page 34 is from the "Random Sampler" article "Update on Gluten" from the *Ensign*, March 1978. All are used by permission of the *Ensign*.

The quote on the preface facing page by Brigham Young is from *The Discourses of Brigham Young*, page 291.

ISBN 0-9658909-1-0

Printing History

1st Printing	September 1995
2nd Printing	July 1996
3rd Printing	March 1998
4th Printing	September 1998
5th Printing	January 1999
Revised edition	April 1999

Dedicated to my family,
whose support made this possible.

"If we are to be saved in an ark, as Noah and his family were,
it will be because we build it."

- Brigham Young

PREFACE

The material in this book comes from years of teaching, study, and practical experience in home storage and preparedness. Most of it was compiled for a series of classes given to help others be preparedness teachers. The information is simple and straight forward, because when preparedness is simplified, it becomes less overwhelming.

I invite you to use this book to learn, to teach, and to become *Simply Prepared*!

TABLE OF CONTENTS

WHAT IF?

CONSIDERING "WHAT IF?"

WHAT IF the primary breadwinner lost his/her job?
  How long could you last financially i.e. savings, storage, skills?
  Could you find a job in your career field?
  Will retraining be necessary?
  Do you have skills and/or hobbies to fall back on?
  Do you know where you can cut back financially?
  Is your consumer debt too high to be manageable?
  Do you have a garden and fruit trees?

WHAT IF the primary breadwinner were disabled?
  How long could you last financially?
  Would you be willing to retrain?
  Do you know where you can cut back financially?
  Is your consumer debt too high to be manageable?
  Do you have disability insurance?

WHAT IF a member of your family had serious health problems?
  Do you have savings to pay for medical bills?
  Do you have medical insurance?
  Could you handle it emotionally?
  Do you have someone to turn to for emotional support?

WHAT IF your family unit were the only church organization?
  Would they be taught well enough?
  Do you have resource materials for teaching?
  Do you understand the gospel well enough to teach your family?
  Would your family church meetings have music?

WHAT IF a hurricane or other major storm hit?
  Do you have emergency supplies - food, water, cash, tools, first aid supplies?
  Do you have property insurance?
  Do you keep at least 1/4 tank of gas in the car at all times?
  Do you have emergency fuel supplies?
  Do you know how to secure your property?

WHAT IF there were an extended shipping strike?
  Do you have HOME storage?
  Do you use your home storage?
  Do you like your home storage?
  Is your food storage nutritionally balanced?
  Do you have a garden and fruit trees?

WHAT IF you have a house fire?
> Do you have insurance?
> Do you have a household inventory stored away from the house?
> Do you have a family escape plan?

WHAT IF your home flooded?
> Do you have flood insurance?
> Do you have a household inventory stored away from the house?
> Do you know how to care for flood damaged goods?
> Do you have enough cleaning supplies to start cleaning up?
> Do you have savings to cover expenses until the insurance checks arrive?

WHAT IF you were without water?
> Do you have emergency water supplies?
> Do you have emergency sanitation materials?
> Do you know how to purify water for drinking?

WHAT IF you were without heat and/or light (power)?
> Could you keep warm?
> Do you have emergency lighting?
> Could you still cook?
> Do you have food that doesn't need cooking?
> Do you know what you would do with your refrigerator and freezer?

WHAT IF you had to evacuate your home?
> Do you have a 72-hr emergency kit?
> Do you have any camping equipment that could be used?
> Do you have a way to locate all family members?
> Do you know the best evacuation route from your home?
> Do you keep at least 1/4 tank of gasoline in your car at all times?

WHAT IF a tornado warning were issued for your area?
> Do you know where to go for protection?
> Do you have a 72-hr emergency kit with a radio?

WHAT IF a tree fell on your house?
> Do you have rope to remove it with?
> Do you have plastic sheeting to cover the damage?
> Do you have access to a chain saw?

WHAT IF Mother were to be gone for a period of time?
> Does the family know how to cook nutritious meals?
> Does the family know how to do laundry?
> Does the family know how to clean house?
> Does the family know how to mend clothes?
> Does the family know how to shop wisely?

WHAT IF your husband passed away?
>What kind and how much insurance does he have?
>Will his benefits support you?
>Will you have to work and are you skilled?
>Where are investments?
>Can you do what he normally does at home?
>Are you spiritually and emotionally prepared to cope?

WHAT IF your wife passed away?
>Could you manage the home?
>What would you do about child care?
>Could you manage without her income if she currently works?
>Does she have life insurance?
>Are you spiritually and emotionally prepared to cope?

WHAT IF you have a serious accident at home?
>Do you have a first aid kit?
>Do you have first aid training?
>Do you know CPR?
>Do you have emergency numbers near the phone?
>Do you know what information to give over the phone?

WHAT IF you have car trouble?
>Do you know how to change a tire?
>Do you know a safe way to get help?
>Do you know how to safely use jumper cables?
>Do you have an emergency car kit?

WHAT IF you have a home utility problem?
>Do you know how to turn off water, gas, and electricity?
>Do you know where the sewer clean out valve is?
>Do you now how to reset circuit breakers?
>Do you know how to light a pilot light?

WHAT IF you were snowed in at home?
>Do you have food and water?
>Could you keep warm?
>Could you communicate with anyone outside of your home?
>Could you clear a way out of your home?
>Could you cope with a power outage, also?

WHAT IF you get stranded at the office overnight?
>Do you have an emergency kit at the office?
>Will you be able to communicate your situation to anyone?

WHAT IF? For Kids

WHAT IF a hurricane hit your city?
   Does your family have 72-hour emergency kits?
   Do you now what to do to protect your house?
   Do you know where to stay in your house?

WHAT IF you had a house fire?
   Do you know how to get out of your house safely?
   Do you know where to meet your family after you are out?

WHAT IF your house flooded?
   Do you know what to save first?
   Do you know what to put upstairs or on a high shelf?
   Do you know what to take with you?

WHAT IF you were without water?
   Does your family have water stored?
   Does someone know how to purify water?
   What would you do without a bathroom to use?

WHAT IF you had no power?
   Do you know where flashlights and/or lanterns are?
   Do you know what you could eat?
   Could you cook?
   Could you stay warm in the winter?

WHAT IF a tornado were coming?
   Do you know where to go for protection if you are inside?
   Do you know where to go for protection if you are outside?
   Do you know the difference between a tornado watch and a tornado warning?

WHAT IF your mom had to be gone for a long time?
   Do you know how to help cook?
   Can you help clean house?
   Can you help do laundry and ironing?
   Can you sew on a button or fix a torn seam?

WHAT IF there were an emergency in your home?
   Do you know who to call?
   Are their telephone numbers easy to find?
   Can you give your complete address over the phone?
   Do you know where the first aid kit is?

THE BASICS

WHY

HOME STORAGE?

Trucking strikes

Natural disasters

Recession

Depression

Crop failures

Drought

Crop destruction

Unemployment

Disability

Unforseen expenses

Death of breadwinner

War

PROPHETIC COUNSEL

"Let every head of every household see to it that he has on hand enough food and clothing, and, where possible, fuel also, for at least a year ahead."
-- J. Rueben Clark, Jr., April 1937

"The revelation to store food may be as essential to our temporal salvation today as boarding the ark was to the people in the days of Noah."
-- Ezra Taft Benson, October 1973

PREPAREDNESS AND THE SCRIPTURES

There are several examples of preparedness in the scriptures:

    1. Noah (Genesis 6-8) - Noah had to take enough food for his family and the animals to last a year plus the time until the next harvest.

    2. Joseph of Egypt (Genesis 41) - Joseph directed the storing of grain during seven plenteous years to be used during seven years of famine.

    3. Moroni, chief commander of the armies of the Nephites (Alma 49:27-50:1) Moroni was successful in defending the cities of Ammonihah and Noah against the Lamanites because he prepared them to be secure. Even after the Lamanites retreated, he continued preparations of defense. "...Moroni had kept the commandments of God in preparing for the safety of his people...And now it came to pass that Moroni did not stop making preparations...to defend his people..."

    4. Nephi, son of Helaman (Helaman 11) - Nephi prayed for a famine to stop war in the land. Famine lasted for three years. Many died "in the more wicked parts of the land." Nephi and his brother Lehi and, we assume, their families survived. Indications would be that the people had a storage program because they did not have forewarning such as Joseph of Egypt. The famine began in the year it was prayed for.

    5. The Nephites governed by Lachoneus (3 Nephi 3-4) - By request of the governor, Lachoneus, the Nephites were directed to gather to Zarahemla in order to battle the Gadianton robbers as one body. They "reserved for themselves provisions, and horses and cattle, and flocks of every kind, that they might subsist for the space of seven years." As a result, "it was impossible for the robbers to lay siege sufficiently long to have any effect upon the Nephites, because of their much provision which they had laid up in store."

I Timothy 5:8
    "But if any provide not for his own, and specially for those of his own house, he hath denied the faith, and is worse than an infidel."

Alma 60:21
    "...do ye suppose that the Lord will still deliver us, while we sit upon our thrones and do not make use of the means which the Lord has provided for us?"

Hebrews 11:7
    "By faith, Noah, being warned of God of things not seen as yet,...,prepared an ark to the saving of his house..."

D&C 88:119
    "Organize yourselves; prepare very needful thing..."

D&C 136:27
    "Thou shalt be diligent in preserving what thou hast, that thou mayest be a wise steward;..."

Proverbs 6:6-8

"Go to the ant, thou sluggard; consider her ways, and be wise: Which having no guide, overseer, or ruler, Provideth her meat in the summer, and gathereth her food in the harvest."

Proverbs 21:20

"There is treasure to be desired and oil in the dwelling of the wise; but a foolish man spendeth it up."

D&C 78:7

"For if you will that I give unto you a place in the celestial world, you must prepare yourselves by doing the things which I have commanded you and required of you."

Luke 6: 46

"And why call ye me, Lord, Lord, and do not the things which I say?"

D&C 1:12

"Prepare ye, prepare ye for that which is to come, for the Lord is nigh:"

D&C 38:30

"...if ye are prepared ye shall not fear."

D&C 29:34

"Wherefore, verily I say unto you that all things unto me are spiritual, and not at any time have I given unto you a law which was temporal..."

I Nephi 3:7

"...I will go and do the things which the Lord hath commanded, for I know that the Lord giveth no commandments unto the children of men, save he shall prepare a way for them that they may accomplish the thing which he commandeth them."

HOME STORAGE AND
HOW TO USE IT

CANNED FOOD COOKBOOKS such as Campbell's, Star-kist, Del Monte, etc.

COOKBOOKS based on whole grains, beans, or vegetarian menus.

COOKIN' WITH HOME STORAGE. Vicki Tate.
> Contains over 500 recipes that use food storage.

COUNTY EXTENSION OFFICES

ESSENTIALS OF HOME PRODUCTION AND STORAGE. The Church of Jesus Christ of Latter-day Saints.
> An excellent and inexpensive basic manual.

HAVING YOUR FOOD STORAGE AND EATING IT, TOO. Ezra Taft Benson Institute. Brigham Young University.
> An excellent basic manual on what and how to store food.

MAKING THE BEST OF BASICS. James Talmage Stevens. Gold Leaf Press.
> A family preparedness handbook.

PANTRY COOKING. Cheryl Driggs.
> Recipes using only storable foods.

SIMPLY PREPARED. Cheryl Driggs. CFD Publications.
> A simple approach to home storage and emergency preparedness.

WORLD WIDE WEB

A YEAR'S SUPPLY. Barry and Lynnette Crockett.
> A guide to help you obtain and store a year's supply of food, clothing, and other necessities.

Check your local bookstore and library for additional titles. Other books may be available depending on the bookstore and the local market.

HOME STORAGE CAUTIONS

Beware what you read; those who advocate the use of whole grains are often fanatical in their views on nutrition.

Learn enough to question something different or unusual, i.e. Vit. B-17, rutin, Vit. B-15, etc.

Natural food stores are good sources for recipes but not necessarily reliable nutrition information.

For current nutrition information, look to sources approved by medical or dietetic associations. Some reliable sources are Jane Brody, *Tufts University Diet and Nutrition Letter, Cooking Light, University of California at Berkeley Wellness Letter* and other major university health newsletters.

Food storage advocates often verge on the fanatical. Fanatical, overbearing people offend and discourage more than they inspire and encourage. As with all things spiritual AND temporal, we only teach food storage and family preparedness when the spirit accompanies our words. The Lord has taught "all things unto me are spiritual, and not at any time have I given unto you a law which was temporal" (D&C 29:34). The temporal and spiritual are interconnected much more than most people realize.

BASIC FOOD STORAGE WORKSHEET

Basic storage is the foundation of any good food storage program. It is composed of life-sustaining foods that store well for long periods. A year's supply of garden seeds for planting should be stored so that the diet may be supplemented with fresh vegetables. Where garden space is limited, a multiple vitamin pill should also be stored for daily use by each person during long periods of emergency. Vitamins deteriorate over time and must be replaced by the expiration date on the container.

The following recommendations are estimated for an average adult and supply 2300 calories per day for 1 year. Amounts for children are a percentage of the adult portion and can be estimated as follows: age 3 and under - 50%; ages 4 to 6 - 70%; ages 7 to 10 - 90%; ages 11 and up - 100%.[1] Instructions for using the worksheet are on page 16.

GRAINS 300 pounds/person

	GOAL	HAVE	NEED
Wheat			
Flour			
Wheat germ			
Bran			
Pancake mix			
Brown rice			
White rice			
Oatmeal			
Oat groats			
Corn			
Cornmeal			
Masa harina			
Popcorn			
Rye			
Buckwheat			
Millet			
Barley			

---

[1] Franz, Kay B. "Food Storage and Children," *Ensign,* March 1998, 71.

	GOAL	HAVE	NEED
Macaroni			
Noodles			
Spaghetti			
Boxed macaroni & cheese			
Other pasta			
Couscous			
Crackers			
Cooked cereals			
Other			
TOTAL			

MILK 75 pounds/person   (50 pounds makes about 60 gallons)

GOAL: HAVE: NEED:

SUGAR, HONEY, & SWEETENERS 60 pounds/person

	GOAL	HAVE	NEED
White sugar			
Brown sugar			
Powdered sugar			
Honey			
Molasses			
Corn syrup			
Pancake syrup			
Jam			
Jelly			
TOTAL			

SALT 5 pounds/person   (1 box = 26 ounces)

GOAL: HAVE: NEED:

FATS   20 pounds/person

	GOAL	HAVE	NEED
Oil			
Shortening			
Dry margarine			
Salad dressing			
Miracle Whip			
Mayonnaise			
TOTAL			

DRIED LEGUMES   60 pounds/person

	GOAL	HAVE	NEED
Pinto beans			
Kidney beans			
White beans			
Garbanzo beans			
Lima beans			
Black beans			
Pink beans			
Blackeye peas			
Soybeans			
Lentils			
Split peas			
Fifteen bean mix			
Refried beans /2			
Canned beans /2			
Chili with beans /2			
Peanut butter			
Other			
TOTAL			

INSTRUCTIONS FOR USING THE
BASIC FOOD STORAGE WORKSHEET

1. Use the recommended amount at the top of each section to determine the total goal amount by multiplying by the number of persons in the family. For example, to determine the total goal amount of grains for a family of 5, multiply 300 pounds by 5 for a goal of 1500 pounds of grains. Enter this number in the GOAL column TOTAL line.

2. Determine how much of each different item you wish to have in order to meet the desired total goal and enter it in the GOAL column on the appropriate line. The chart, Basic Food Weight Equivalents, can help you figure a minimum amount of specific foods based on your current usage.

3. Inventory your food storage and enter the amounts on the appropriate lines in the HAVE column.

4. Subtract the amount in the HAVE column from the amount in the GOAL column for each line to determine the amount still needed and enter it in the NEED column.

5. Make a plan for acquiring items in the NEED column in a specific amount of time.

GRAINS
    Whole grains provide fiber, vitamins, and trace minerals, including iron, which are not always found in processed or refined grains. When grains are a major part of the diet, eating whole instead of refined grains will make a difference nutritionally. Whole grains can also be sprouted. Therefore, at least sixty-five percent of the grains should be whole grains. The remaining thirty-five percent can be processed or refined grains and grain products, if desired, but any whole grain that is altered has a shorter shelf life.

MILK
    This is the most expensive part of food storage and has only a 2 to 3 year shelf life. Buy only what you use, even if it less than the recommended amount, to avoid waste. Recent studies have shown that less milk can be stored and used if more grains are stored and used. Store one 50-lb. bag for every gallon of milk you use in a week. For example, if your family drinks 4 gallons of milk a week, store four 50-lb. bags or 200 lbs. of milk.

SALT
    At least half of the salt stored should be iodized.
    Canning or pickling salt contains none of the additives found in table salt that keep it free flowing. It is better for canning and pickling since it produces a clear rather than a cloudy liquid.

Use the following chart to determine how many 26 ounce cylinder boxes of salt to store:

# people	# boxes
1	3
2	7
3	10
4	13
5	16
6	19
7	22
8	25

LEGUMES

Because dry beans approximately double when cooked, one pound of cooked or canned beans does not equal one pound of dry beans. Instead, one pound of canned beans equals about one half pound of dry beans. When figuring amounts of canned beans into the total, this must be considered. Therefore, /2 (divided by 2) is on the worksheet to remind you that you must divide by two to determine how many pounds of dry beans you really have.

NOTE: Variety need not be limited to what is on the worksheet. If other items fit into any of the categories, add them to the list. Remember to store only what you and your family will eat. Eat what you store and store what you eat. If you do not use something from your storage every day, you are storing the wrong things.

When basic storage is becoming complete, start on expanded storage. Expanded storage would include foods that supply total nutritional needs, add variety, and allow for personal preferences. This would include items normally used each day, such as baking powder, spices, and canned fruits and vegetables. It is wise to first obtain fruits and vegetables high in vitamins A and C and food items that make the basics more versatile. Each person should have a minimum of 2 cups of fruits and vegetables each day.

VITAMIN A
Tomatoes
Tomato soup
Tomato juice
Tomato sauce
Tomato paste
Spinach and other greens
Yams
Vegetable soup
Carrots
Apricots
Pumpkin
Mixed vegetables
Peas (not dried)
Squash
Peaches

VITAMIN C
Tomatoes
Tomato soup
Tomato juice
Tomato sauce
Tomato paste
Spinach and other greens
Sweet potatoes
Orange breakfast drink
Orange juice
Enriched juices
Mandarin oranges
Corn
Pineapple juice
Peppers

Recommendations for the amounts of basic foods to store are based on information from ESSENTIALS OF HOME PRODUCTION AND STORAGE published by The Church of Jesus Christ of Latter-day Saints.

BASIC FOOD
WEIGHT EQUIVALENTS

Barley, pearled

1 pound = 2 cups
1 cup dry = 4 cups cooked

Beans, kidney

1 pound dry = 2-1/2 cups
1 pound dry = 5-1/2 cups cooked
15.5 ounce can = 2 cups cooked

, lima

1 pound dry = 2-1/2 cups
1 pound dry = 5-1/2 cups cooked
15.5 ounce can = 2 cups cooked

, navy (pea)

1 pound dry = 2 cups
1 pound dry = 5 cups cooked

, soy

1 pound dry = 2 cups
1 pound dry = 6 cups cooked

, white

1 pound dry = 2 cups
1 pound dry = 6 cups cooked

Blackeye peas

1 pound dry = 2 cups
1 pound dry = 6 cups cooked
15.5 ounce can = 2 cups cooked

Bulgur

1 pound = 2-2/3 cups
1 cup = 6 ounces
1 cup, cooked = 3 cups

Corn flour

1 pound = 4 cups

Cornmeal, white
        , yellow

1 pound = 3-1/2 cups
1 pound = 3 cups
1 cup = 5-1/2 cups cooked

Corn syrup

16 fluid ounces = 2 cups

Flour, all purpose

1 pound = 4 cups sifted
1 pound = 3-1/2 cups unsifted

, cake

1 pound = 4-3/4 cups sifted
1 pound = 4-1/4 cups unsifted

, whole wheat
, rice
, rye

1 pound = 3-1/3 to 4 cups finely milled and stirred
1 pound = 3-1/2 cups
1 pound = 5 cups

Honey

1 pound = 1-1/3 cups

Lentils

1 pound = 2-1/4 cups dry
1 pound dry = 5 cups cooked

Macaroni, elbow

1 pound dry = 4-1/2 cups cooked
1 cup dry = 2 cups cooked

, shell	1 pound dry = 4-1/2 cups cooked
	1 cup dry = 2 cups cooked
Milk, evaporated	5 ounces = less than 2/3 cup
	12 ounces = 1-1/2 cups
, instant dry	1 pound = 6 cups
	1 pound reconstituted = 4-1/2 quarts
, non-instant dry	1 pound = 3-1/3 cups
	1 pound reconstituted = 5 quarts
	50 pounds reconstituted = 62-1/2 gallons
Molasses	12 fluid ounce jar = 1-1/2 cups
Noodles	1 pound = 8 to 12 cups
	1 cup dry = 1-1/3 cups cooked
	12 ounces medium noodles = 6 cups
	1 pound medium noodles = 8 cups
	12 ounces broad noodles = 7 cups
	1 pound broad noodles = 9-1/3 cups
Oats, old fashioned	1 pound = 4-1/2 cups
	1 cup dry = 1-3/4 cups cooked
, quick	1 pound = 5-1/3 cups
	18 ounce box = 6 cups
	42 ounce box = 14 cups
	1 cup dry = 3 ounces
	1 cup dry = 1-3/4 cups cooked
Oil	32 ounces = 4 cups
Peanut butter	8.9 ounces = 1 cup
	18 ounces = 2 cups
	1 pound = 1-3/4 cups
Peas, dried split	1 pound = 2-1/4 cups
	1 pound dried = 5 cups cooked
Popcorn	1 pound = 3 cups
	1/4 cup dry = 5 cups popped
Rice	1 cup uncooked = 3 cups cooked
	1 cup instant, uncooked = 2 cups cooked
	1 cup instant brown, uncooked = 2 cups cooked
	1 cup wild uncooked = 3-1/2 to 4 cups cooked
	1 pound long grain = 2-1/2 cups
	1 pound medium grain = 2-1/3 cups
	1 pound short grain = 2-1/4 cups
	1 pound brown = 2-1/2 cups
	1 pound instant = 5-1/3 cups
	1 pound wild = 2-2/3 cups

Salt	1 box = 26 ounces
	26 ounces = scant 2-1/2 cups
	1 pound = 1-1/2 cups
Shortening	1 pound = 2-1/3 cups
Spaghetti	1 pound dry = 5 cups
	1 pound dry = 8 cups cooked
Sugar	1 cup granulated = 7 ounces
	1 pound granulated = 2 to 2-1/2 cups
	1 pound light brown, packed = 2-1/4 cups
	1 pound dark brown, packed = 2 to 2-1/2 cups
	1 pound granulated brown = 3-3/4 cups
	1 pound powdered = 3-1/3 to 4 cups
	1 pound powdered, sifted = 4-1/2 cups
Wheat, whole	1 cup = 1-2/3 cups flour
	5 cups = 8 cups flour
	7 cups = 11 cups flour

A MONTH'S SUPPLY

Based on suggested amounts in "Essentials of Home Production and Storage," a month's supply of food for one person would consist of the following:

Grains	25 pounds
Powdered milk	6.25 pounds
Sugar or honey	5 pounds
Salt	1/4 box
Fats and oils	1-2/3 pounds
Legumes	5 pounds

A suggested month's supply of food for one person could consist of the following foods:

One case of 6 #10 cans* - 1 can wheat (about 6 pounds)
                                           1 can rice (about 6 pounds)
                                           1 can rolled oats or macaroni (about 3 pounds)
                                           1 can popcorn (about 6 pounds)
                                           1 can non-instant non-fat dry milk (about 4 pounds)
                                           1 can dry beans (5 pounds)

5 pound bag flour
4 or 5 pound bag sugar
26 ounce box salt
32 ounce bottle oil

ESTIMATED COST: less than $20

"It is...necessary that each home and family do what they can to assume the responsibility for their own hour of need. If we do not have the resources to acquire a year's supply, then we can strive to begin with having one month's supply."

--James E. Faust, April 1986

---

* Where facilities and equipment are unavailable for canning these items, purchase the equivalent amount and store in a container with a tight fitting lid. (See pages 30 and 31.)

WHY BASICS FIRST?

Basic food storage should include 300 pounds of grains, 60 pounds of dry beans, 20 pounds of fats and oils, 60 pounds of honey and sugars, 75 pounds of dry milk, and 5 pounds of salt per adult. These should be the first foods stored for the following reasons:

1. LONG SHELF LIFE - except for powdered milk, unrefined basic storage foods will store indefinitely when kept dry, dark, airtight, and at 70 degrees or below. Higher temperatures shorten shelf life, but foods will still last longer than canned goods stored the same way.

2. THEY ARE THE LEAST EXPENSIVE FOODS - a year's supply of basic foods for an adult costs $200 to $250. A year's supply of any other kind or combination of foods cost $500 to $3900 per adult.

3. THEY PROVIDE THE MOST NUTRITION FOR THE VOLUME - basic foods are dry foods except for the fats and oils. Water is necessary for many of them to be cooked and/or eaten. Therefore, the space necessary for storage is much less than canned goods which have liquid in addition to the food.

4. THEY PROVIDE ALL BUT VITAMINS A & C - even these vitamins can be provided by unusual grains such as amaranth. Sprouting can also provide small amounts. It is best, though, to store vitamins and/or garden seeds for fresh vegetables until a supply of canned fruits and vegetables can be maintained.

5. THEY ARE THE BASIS OF A HEALTHY DISEASE PREVENTION DIET - current nutrition and health research indicates that the healthiest diets are low fat, high fiber, high complex carbohydrate diets. Whole grains, legumes, and low-fat milk are all a part of this diet.

FOOD SOURCES

1. Grocery stores

2. Wholesale clubs

3. Natural food stores

4. LDS Church canneries

    Food items purchased must be dry-packed before they are taken home. OR dry packing equipment may be checked out to use at your home.

5. Food co-ops

    Individuals may join a co-op for a fee and some shared labor in order to be able to buy bulk items at a lower price.

6. Mail order

    Sources are often listed in wholefood or natural food cookbooks and emergency preparedness books.

To members of The Church of Jesus Christ of Latter-day Saints:

Wards, stakes, and quorums are not to be involved in buying and selling food and nonfood commodities for storage purposes. Individuals may work together to buy and sell food and nonfood commodities for storage purposes, but such activities should not be Church-sponsored in ANY way.

--Welfare Services Resource Handbook, p. 19

Wards and stakes are not to enter into a buying and selling program to their members,...

--Harold B. Lee, Welfare meeting, Oct 1966.

Merchandising activities not related to the exempt purposes of the Church are not to be conducted by stakes, wards, or quorums. Stakes, wards, and quorums are not to be involved in purchasing and selling items such as food, storage containers, or nonreligious books. If individuals or groups wish to form independent organizations to obtain group discounts on home storage items, they may do so. These independent groups should abide by local laws and should not be identified with the Church.

--Essentials of Home Production and Storage, p. 9

HOLD ON TO YOUR SEEDS

If stored properly, opened and unused seeds can be saved for later planting.

Leftover seeds are often stored in a drawer or other area where they are unprotected from heat and moisture. Under those conditions, the metabolic processes within the seeds speed up and cause rapid deterioration. Even in a year, the seeds may not germinate. Proper storage in cool, dry conditions slows down metabolic activity, preserving seed energy until planting time.

The best place to store seeds at home is in the refrigerator. But before placing them in the refrigerator, put the seeds (in packets or loose) in a sealed container, such as airtight plastic canisters, jars, or freezer bags. Under these conditions, they are safe from the detrimental effects of heat and moisture.

Seeds and seed packets must be dry when stored; otherwise, they will provide a source of moisture during storage. Moist seeds in a sealed container will deteriorate even faster than dry ones that are left in unprotected storage. Two teaspoons of powdered milk or silica gel added to the containers of seeds will absorb any excess moisture. These materials may be packaged in a small piece of thin fabric. It is best not to use dry milk or silica gel when storing seeds of corn, okra, or beans, as overdrying may result.

When stored under cool, dry conditions, seeds should remain viable for the following number of years from the time of harvest (not time of purchase):

VEGETABLE	YEARS	VEGETABLE	YEARS
Asparagus	3	Lettuce	5
Beans	3	Mustard	4
Beets	4	Okra	3
Blackeye peas	3	Onion	1
Broccoli	4	Parsley	1-2
Brussel sprouts	4	Parsnips	1-2
Cabbage	4	Peas	3
Cantaloupe	5	Pepper	3
Carrots	3	Pumpkin	4
Cauliflower	4	Radish	4
Celery	5	Rutabaga	4
Collards	4	Spinach	4
Corn	1-2	Squash	4
Cucumber	5	Swiss chard	4
Eggplant	5	Tomato	3
Endive	5	Turnip	4
Kale	4	Watermelon	5
Kohlrabi	4		

To test questionable seeds, run a germination test. A few weeks before planting, sandwich 10 seeds in a paper towel and keep it moist (not wet). If at least 7 seeds sprout, the seeds are approximately the same as new seeds.

REFERENCE: SOUTHERN LIVING MAGAZINE and THE TIGHTWAD GAZETTE

AFFORDING HOME STORAGE

1. Make home storage a regular budget item.
2. Use your income tax return.
3. Use bonuses.
4. Have a home storage Christmas.
5. Grow a garden and can the extra produce.
6. Use bulk purchases for regular monthly groceries and use the money saved for home storage.
7. Use checking account interest.
8. Shop sales and stock up.
9. Follow the counsel by Vaughn J. Featherstone in April 1976 General Conference.

"Now you ask, 'Where do I get the money for these things? I agree we need them, but I'm having a hard time making ends meet.'

Here is how you do it. Use any one or all of these suggestions, some of which may not be applicable in your country:

1. Decide as a family this year that 25 or 50 percent of your Christmas will be spent on a year's supply. Many families in the Church spend considerable sums of money for Christmas. Half or part of these Christmas monies will go a long way toward purchasing the basics. I recall the Scotsman who went to the doctor and had an x-ray taken of his chest. Then he had the x-ray gift-wrapped and gave it to his wife for their anniversary. He couldn't afford a gift, but he wanted her to know his heart was in the right place. Brethren, give your wife a year's supply of wheat for Christmas, and she'll know your heart is in the right place.

2. When you desire new clothes, don't buy them. Repair and mend and make your present wardrobe last a few months longer. Use that money for the food basics. Make all of your nonfood necessities that you feasibly can, such as furniture and clothing.

3. Cut the amount of money you spend on recreation by 50 percent. Do fun things that do not require money outlay but make more lasting impressions on your children.

4. Decide as a family that there will be no vacation or holiday next year unless you have your year's supply. Many Church members could buy a full year's supply of the basics from what they would save by not taking a vacation. Take the vacation time and work on a family garden. Be together, and it can be just as much fun.

5. If you haven't a year's supply yet and you do have boats, snowmobiles, campers, or other luxury possessions, sell or trade one or two or more of them and get your year's supply.

6. Watch advertised specials in the grocery stores and pick up extra supplies of those items that are of exceptional value.

7. Change the mix in your family's diet. Get your protein from sources less expensive than meat. The grocery bill is one bill that can be cut. Every time you enter the store and feel tempted by effective and honest merchandising to buy cookies, candy, ice cream, non-food items, or magazines -- don't! Think carefully: buy only the essentials. Then figure what you have saved and spend it on powdered milk, sugar, honey, salt, or grain.

The Lord will make it possible, if we make a firm commitment, for every Latter-day Saint family to have a year's supply of food reserves...All we have to do is to decide, commit to do it, and then keep the commitment. Miracles will take place: the way will be opened, and... we will have our storage areas filled. We will prove through our actions our willingness to follow our beloved prophet and the Brethren, which will bring security to us and our families."

SHELF LIFE

Ideal storage conditions are cool (below 70°F), dry, dark, and airtight. Less than ideal conditions, especially higher temperatures, shorten shelf life. Shelf life indicates when quality BEGINS to deteriorate. Times indicated are for products without a "Use by" date on them. Date cans and bottles according to purchase date to know how long they have been stored.

FOOD	TIME
Baking powder	18 months
Baking soda	2 years
Bouillon cubes	18 months
Cake mixes	12 months
Casserole mixes	18 months
Catsup	2 years
Cereal, cooked	2+ years
, ready to eat	6-12 months
Chili sauce	2 years
Chocolate	1 year
Cocoa mixes	8+ months
Coconut	1 year
Cornmeal	1+ years
Cornstarch	18 months
Crackers	6 months
Dehydrated foods	1+ years
Eggs, dried	1-2 years
Extracts	1 year
Flour, whole wheat	1 year
, white	2+ years
Fruits, canned, high acid (grapefruit juice, orange juice, cherries, berries, prunes, plums, cranberry sauce, rhubarb)	18 months
Fruits, canned, other	3+ years
Gelatin	18 months
Gravy mix	6-12 months

Herbs and spices	
whole spices	3-5 years
ground spices	3-5 years
herbs	6 months
Honey	Indefinite
Jams, jellies	18 months
Legumes, dried	Indefinite
Meats, canned	2+ years
Milk, condensed	1 year
, evaporated	1 year
, instant dry	2 years
, non-instant dry	2 years
Molasses	2+ years
Mustard	2 years
Nuts	9 months
Oil	2+ years
Olives	2 years
Pancake mix	6-9 months
Pasta	2+ years
Peanut butter, jar	9-12 months
, crunchy, can	9-12 months
, creamy, can	18-24 months
Pickles	18 months
Pie filling	1 year
Pimientos	3 years
Potatoes, instant	18 months
Potato chips, canned	1-2 years
Pudding mixes	1 year
Rice, white	2+ years
, brown	1-2 years
, wild	indefinite
Rice mixes	6 months
Salad dressings	12-18 months
Salt	Indefinite
Sauce mixes	6-12 months
Seafood, canned	18 months

Shortening	Indefinite
Soups, canned	3 years
, dried	1 year
Soy protein extracts (TVP)	18-24 months
Sugar	Indefinite
Syrup	1+ years
Tabasco	2+ years
Tuna	2+ years
Vanilla	2 years
Vegetables, canned, sauerkraut	18 months
, beets	2 years
, tomatoes, sweet potatoes, spinach, mushrooms, potatoes, pumpkin	2+ years
, asparagus, green beans, hominy	3 years
, peas, corn, carrots	3+ years
, lima beans	4 years
, squash	4+ years
Vinegar	2 years
Wheat	Indefinite
Whipped topping mix	1 year
Worcestershire sauce	2+ years
Yeast, dry	18-24 months

HOW TO STORE

COOL - Store food inside. Temperature affects shelf life the most. Canned goods store 2 to 3 times longer at 70°F than they do at 90°F. Most dry goods store indefinitely below 70°F but for less time at higher temperatures. Temperature affects nutrition, texture, and taste.

DRY - Dry goods should be below 10% moisture and kept dry. The more a container is opened, the more moisture is introduced. The humidity in the air the day food is dry packed or "home canned" can also affect the storage life. Weevil cannot grow in grain with less than 10% moisture. Beans with less than 10% moisture won't go hard as quickly. Non-fat dry milk should have no more than 2.8% moisture for the longest life.

DARK - Store in opaque containers or in dark cupboards. Light fades colors, destroys vitamins, and speeds the rancidity of fats.

AIRTIGHT - Containers should have airtight seams and lids. If in doubt, seal with duct tape. Plastic buckets with rubber gaskets are airtight if the gasket has not been damaged. Insects cannot grow and multiply without air.

THE BATTLE OF THE BUGS

If food is infested with weevil, it may be treated two ways. Adult insects can be destroyed by placing the food in a freezer at or below 15°F for 2 to 3 days. This may not kill all the larvae and eggs so repeat this process after a month. All insects, eggs, and larvae will be killed if frozen at 10°F for 2 to 3 days.

Insects can also be destroyed by heat. Heat the grain, layered 3/4 inch deep, on a pan in an oven at 150°F for 20 minutes. Higher temperatures and longer periods of time will reduce germination and, perhaps, handling quality of subsequent flour milled from the grain.

DON'T "BAG" IT

Plastic trash bags should not be used to store wheat. According to reports, some chemical residues migrate from this type of plastic into the wheat. If you've already stored in this manner, you probably do not need to discard the wheat; simply transfer it to other appropriate containers.
--Clayton S. Huber, Brigham Young University

STORAGE CONTAINERS

Dry goods may be stored in several types of storage containers:

PLASTIC
1. Plastic should be food grade plastic.
2. Opaque containers are preferable to translucent containers.
3. The containers must be air tight (preferably with a rubber gasket in the lid).
4. Containers should not be in direct contact with the floor and should be stored away from sun light.
5. Used containers may be utilized for storage if they previously stored food, no odor persists from the previous contents, and if lids still seal air tight (gaskets should be intact).
6. Plastic containers should not be stored in areas with gasoline, paint thinner, paint rags, etc., as fumes from these may penetrate the containers and contaminate the food.
7. Plastic should be used with caution in areas infested with large rodents that might chew through the containers.

METAL
1. The lids and containers should be air tight. Side seams should have a continuous weld. Cans with "paint lip" lids are best. Containers, or lids that are not air tight should be taped with duct tape to make them air tight.
2. Containers should be stored so that air circulates under them.
3. In high humidity areas, the cans should be painted with a rust inhibiting paint.
4. Large metal garbage cans and drums are generally too large to be convenient storage containers.

OTHER
1. Plastic bags are not effective for long term storage of dry goods. Also, they are not necessary as liners in other storage containers. Colored bags may "bleed" chemicals into the food.
2. Cardboard boxes and barrels or paper bags are not effective for long term storage because they are not air or moisture tight nor pest resistant.
3. Glass jars can be used if stored away from light, lids are tight, and jars can be kept from breaking.
4. Mylar bags are effective if an oxygen absorber is used or if they are vacuum packed. Bags should be 7 ml thick to avoid puncturing from minor abrasion and to protect from rodents.

CONTAINER SIZE CHART

CONTAINER SIZE	Pounds of Food Container Will Hold			
	GROUP 1	GROUP 2	GROUP 3	GROUP 4
1 gallon	7 lbs	5 lbs	4 lbs	3 lbs
2 gallon	15 lbs	10 lbs	8 lbs	6 lbs
4 gallon	30 lbs	20 lbs	15 lbs	13 lbs
5 gallon	35 lbs	25 lbs	20 lbs	15 lbs
6.5 gal.	50 lbs	30 lbs	25 lbs	20 lbs
13 gallon	100 lbs	60 lbs	50 lbs	40 lbs
30 gallon	225 lbs	150 lbs	120 lbs	90 lbs
55 gallon	400 lbs	275 lbs	225 lbs	160 lbs

Group 1: Wheat, beans, rice, sugar, grains
Group 2: Non-instant powdered milk, flour
Group 3: Oatmeal, macaroni, spaghetti
Group 4: Instant powdered milk, potato flakes

"CANNING" WITH DRY ICE

When dry foods are purchased in large quantities, they must be stored properly in order to remain edible and pest free. One method of storage is "canning" with dry ice.

Dry ice is solidified carbon dioxide. Care should be taken when handling it to avoid burns. Hands should be protected by cloth or leather gloves or folded paper when handling it. (Check the yellow pages under "Dry Ice" for sources.)

At room temperature, dry ice will sublimate or turn to gas from its solid form. When dry ice is placed in a container of food, the resultant carbon dioxide forces the oxygen and free moisture out of the container. The remaining atmosphere suffocates insects but will not kill any eggs in the food. If the container is kept sealed and airtight, the carbon dioxide will remain and the eggs will not hatch. Repeated openings will allow air and moisture to return, though, and eggs will then hatch.

When "canning" with dry ice, approximately 8 ounces of ice is required for 100 pounds of grain; two ounces (about a 2-inch cube) per 5 gallon bucket. Place 1 to 2 inches of food in the bottom of the container. Add the dry ice and then pour food over the dry ice to fill the container. Place the lid on loosely. Wait one hour before sealing the lid on. If the container begins to bulge, "pop" the lid and wait a little longer. An un-"popped" container will explode. Then, be sure the container is airtight before it is stored or carbon dioxide will be lost.

Avoid placing dry ice directly on plastic. The extreme cold could cause the plastic to become brittle and crack. Also, do not use glass containers. The pressure of the gas could cause the glass to shatter.

DRY HEAT PROCESSING

FOR: Grains and grain products
      Dehydrated foods
      Nuts, cocoa, etc.

Fill clean, dry canning jars with food. Place open jars in a 200° F oven. Leave the oven door ajar to allow moisture to escape. Leave quarts 20 minutes; pints 10 minutes. Remove hot jars from the oven. Put clean canning lids and rings on the jars while they are still hot. Allow to cool. The lid will seal, but a vacuum will not form in most jars so the lid will still push in when it is pressed. As long as the lids seal, the jars will be airtight.

WHERE DO I PUT IT ALL?

1. Under beds in boxes or on cardboard flats for easy retrieval.

2. Under baby cribs hidden by a long dust ruffle.

3. Between a bed head board and wall.

4. Between the couch and the wall.

5. Along the wall of a closet underneath hanging clothes.

6. Build a false wall with slanted shelves behind it that are one can height wide. Roll cans in the upper end; take them out on the lower end.

7. Cut out wall board between wall studs. Insert shallow shelves and put a cabinet door over it.

8. Locate unused space under stairs and behind walls of second story rooms. Cut a doorway, finish off walls and floors and put a vent in the wall.

9. Stack boxes or buckets. Put on a round tabletop and cover with a cloth for an end table or decorative accent table.

10. Mount 12″ deep shelves, floor to ceiling, along a wall. Cover with drapes hung from the ceiling.

11. Build bookcases for books and/or toys out of boards and food storage buckets or boxes.

12. Add an extra shelf above the existing shelf in a closet.

13. Convert an extra closet or half of a large closet to shelves - built in or free standing.

14. Replace kitchen soffiting with cabinets.

15. Use the unused back spaces in corner cupboards.

16. Buy a free standing cabinet or armoire; add extra shelving if necessary.

FOOD BASICS

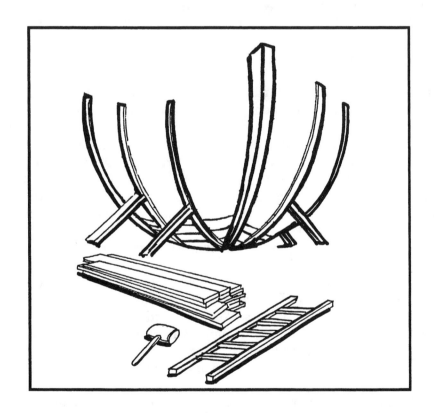

GRAINS

GRAINS should have 10% or less moisture to store well.

WHEAT, sometimes called "wheat berries," should be #1 grade (not less than 60 lbs. per bushel) hard winter wheat or hard spring wheat of 12-16% protein. It should be cleaned for human consumption (usually triple cleaned) and free from foreign particles or materials.

Testing "old" WHEAT (try both before considering discarding the wheat)
1. Sprout 100 kernels of wheat. If 50 or more sprout, the wheat is still good.
2. Grind the wheat into flour and make bread. If the bread rises and bakes well, the wheat is still good.

1 cup whole grain wheat = 1-2/3 cups whole wheat flour

BREAD FLOUR is flour with a higher percentage of protein than all-purpose flour. Therefore, bread can be made with less flour and still produce a good structure when it is baked. It is flour from hard wheat, whereas, all-purpose flour is a mixture of hard and soft wheats.

HARD WHEAT - high-gluten wheat generally used as bread flour.

SOFT WHEAT - low-gluten wheat used for pastry flour.

DURUM WHEAT - very hard spring wheat used for pasta and couscous.

WHITE WHEAT - usually refers to hard white spring wheat. It is lighter in color and flavor than hard red wheats and bakes into a lighter textured product.

BULGUR - whole wheat that has been steamed, dried, and then cracked.

"GLUTEN making is a novel process of extracting the major proteins from wheat flour by washing away the starch granules after the dough is developed. Unfortunately the wheat germ, which is higher in nutrition, is also washed away, as are most of the water soluble B vitamins and the small percentage of water soluble protein in the wheat. As the wheat kernel protein is not a high quality protein to begin with, the loss of the wheat germ protein and the water soluble protein is significant.

Though somewhat wasteful of nutrients, time, and food, using gluten is not a harmful practice unless people get the wrong idea of using it as a meat substitute. It has approximately one-half the quality of meat protein in sustaining growing children."

--Dr. Hal Johnson, Brigham Young University

LONG GRAIN RICE - The most popular rice in the United States. It is usually enriched with powdered niacin, thiamin, and iron. Do not rinse before using.

CONVERTED RICE - White rice that has been soaked, steamed, and dried before the hull is removed. It retains slightly more nutrients than regular white rice. It is not precooked and may require more cooking time and more liquid than standard white rice.

INSTANT RICE - Rice that has been completely cooked and dried. It rehydrates when soaked in boiling water.

BROWN RICE - Rice that retains the grain's bran, but not its hull. Nutritionally, brown rice is similar to enriched white varieties, except that it contains slightly more trace minerals and a bit more fat. It also has up to three times more fiber--about 2 grams per half-cup serving.

WILD RICE - not actually a rice, but the seed of an aquatic grass.

PEARL BARLEY - has the outer hull, most of the bran, and some of the germ removed.

HULLED BARLEY (Scotch or Pot barley) - less processed than pearl barley. Requires a longer cooking time.

HULLESS BARLEY - cultivated so that the hull comes off more easily and does not require polishing or "pearling."

DENT CORN - a variety of corn used for cornmeal, animal feed and hominy.

INDIAN CORN - ancient varieties of corn usually in colors other than yellow.

POPCORN - the only corn variety that will pop because of its hard outer covering and low moisture content. Can also be ground into cornmeal.

OAT GROATS - whole grain oats.

STEEL-CUT OATS (Irish or Scotch oats) - oat groats that have been cut into 2 or 3 pieces with a steel blade.

ROLLED OATS (Old-fashioned oats) - oat groats that have been steamed and rolled flat.

QUICK OATS - steel cut oats that have been steamed and rolled flat. They are thinner and cook faster than rolled oats.

OAT FLAKES - similar to rolled oats but thicker.

AMARANTH - the tiny seed of a broadleaf plant native to Central America. It is high in protein and fiber and contains Vitamin C.

BUCKWHEAT - the triangular seed of a leafy plant. Roasted buckwheat is called kasha.

JOB'S TEARS - an ancient grain highly regarded in the Far East. It looks like a large pearl barley or a small white bean.

KAMUT - an ancient variety of wheat sometimes called Egyptian wheat.

MILLET - a round yellow seed used throughout the world since ancient times. In the U.S., it is most commonly used as birdseed.

QUINOA (KEEN-wah) - a small flat round seed native to the Andes Mountains and used anciently by Aztec and Mayan Indians. It is one of the few grains that is a complete protein.

RYE - similar to wheat but contains less gluten. It is darker in color and stronger in flavor than wheat.

SPELT - similar to wheat and thought to be an ancestor of modern day hybrid wheats. High in gluten, it may be used like wheat in baking. People with wheat allergies are often able to eat spelt.

TEFF - the tiniest grain. It is a highly nutritious ancient grain still commonly used in Ethiopia.

TRITICALE - a cross between wheat and rye. It has less gluten than wheat but more than rye.

BEANS

Beans may be soaked overnight or the quick soak method may be used. Bring beans and water to a boil and boil 2 minutes. Remove from heat and let stand 1 hour. Proceed with cooking as though beans were soaked overnight.

Baking soda may be added when soaking and cooking beans in hard water to help them cook to a softer texture. Add no more than 1/4 teaspoon per pot during the soaking period. Any more will destroy the thiamine in the beans.

According to Dr. Joseph Rackis of the USDA, flatulence from legumes results when undigested complex sugars in the lower intestine are acted upon by naturally occurring bacteria. These complex sugars (called trisaccharides) are water soluble, and soaking and frequent rinsing of the beans wash them away.

Some ways to cut the physical discomfort associated with beans are as follows:
•Some beans are less gas-producing and some more. This varies from person to person, but in general, adzuki beans, mung beans, split peas, lima beans, and lentils are the most digestible.
•Discard the soaking water and cook the beans in fresh water.
•Sprouting helps due to the rinsing done during the sprouting process.
•Eat beans more often. Those who eat beans infrequently are more troubled with flatulence. There is greater intestinal tolerance after three weeks of eating beans regularly.
•Eat smaller amounts per serving.
•Drink more fluids.
•Chewing well and slowly helps minimize the problem.
•Getting plenty of exercise improves your digestion in general.

Do not mix newly purchased beans with older beans. Since older beans take longer to cook, mixing will result in uneven cooking.

Moisture content above 10% and heat speed up hardening of stored beans. When beans become hard they will not soften by soaking and cooking. When this happens, crack them as you would crack corn or grain. This can be done in a hand grinder or by placing the beans in a heavy paper sack and pounding them with the side of a hammer. After cracking, soak and cook them.

Salt and season beans AFTER cooking. Salt, especially, will slow the absorption of water and the softening of the beans.

HONEY AND SUGAR

To substitute honey for sugar in recipes, reduce the liquid by 1/4 cup for each cup of honey used. In baked goods, also add 1/2 tsp. baking soda for each cup of honey used and bake approximately 25 degrees lower.

Honey that can crystallize stores better than honey that cannot since the high sugar concentration prevents fermentation and the growth of microorganisms. For honey to crystallize, the water content must be below 18%. Look for Grade A Pure honey.

If you buy honey in large containers such as five-gallon buckets, pour it into smaller containers to store. It will be easier to liquefy the honey after it crystallizes if it is in smaller containers. Glass jars are preferable to cans since the acid in the honey sometimes interacts with metal in the can and causes a black discoloration.

To liquefy honey, place the open container in a pan of warm water and heat (do not boil) until the honey is completely liquefied. Heating to high temperatures can cause undesirable flavor changes. Leaving any crystals in the honey will cause it to recrystallize faster. Allow to cool before replacing the lid.

HONEY	SUGAR
81% sugar (fructose and glucose)	99.5% sucrose (fructose bonded to glucose)
About 17-20% water	About 1% water
65 calories per tablespoon	45 calories per tablespoon
21 grams per tablespoon	12 grams per tablespoon
Nutritionally insignificant amounts of protein, calcium, phosphorus, iron, potassium, thiamine, riboflavin, niacin, and vitamin C	Nutritionally insignificant amounts of iron and potassium
Will darken and flavor will become stronger after time	May start browning but has no taste change
Will eventually crystallize	Remains free from lumps if stored dry
Loses flavor and aroma with sustained air exposure	
Acid content increases with time	
Cost is about 4 to 6 times more than sugar	Cost is much less than honey

NONFAT DRY MILK

INSTANT MILK - 1-1/3 cups powder/ quart water
NON-INSTANT MILK - 2/3 cups powder/ quart water

50 pounds of non-fat dry milk yields 60 or more gallons of fluid milk. There will be twice as much instant powder as non-instant powder in volume.

TO MIX NON-INSTANT: Combine 4 cups water with 2/3 cup dry milk and beat with beater or blender until smooth. Refrigerate. Makes 1 quart.
Alternate method: Pour 2 cups lukewarm water into a quart jar. Add 2/3 cups dry milk; cap the jar and shake until mixed. Add water to make one quart and stir. Refrigerate immediately.

IN COOKING: Nonfat dry milk can be used as a substitute for whole milk in most recipes. Add dry milk powder to the dry ingredients and add the same amount of water as liquid milk called for in the recipe. The nonfat dry milk may also be reconstituted first and used as one would use fresh milk.

A teaspoon of vanilla added to a gallon of reconstituted milk will often convince finicky drinkers to drink powdered milk.

When using powdered milk to make yogurt, make the milk with twice as much powder.

Non-instant or regular non-fat dry milk should be less than 4% moisture. For the longest storage, moisture should be no greater than 2.8% It should be low heat spray process and enriched, if possible.

Powdered milk should be stored airtight, dark, dry and cool. It is quite heat sensitive. Heat causes a chemical reaction between the milk protein and milk sugar. The milk starts to turn light brown, change in flavor and the protein quality is reduced. Dry milk should be used within two to three years even when stored under favorable conditions.

6 cans (12 oz. each) of evaporated milk are equivalent to 1 pound of dry milk.

1 cup milk = 1/2 cup evaporated milk + 1/2 cup water

Cost comparison Winter 1999

Name brand whole milk	$ 4.09/ gallon
Name brand skim milk	4.09/ gallon
Store brand whole milk	2.27/ gallon
Store brand skim milk	2.27/ gallon
Name brand evaporated milk (reconst.)	4.16/ gallon
Store brand evaporated milk (reconst.)	3.09/ gallon
Name brand instant powdered	2.48/ gallon
Store brand instant powdered	1.96/ gallon
Non-instant powdered	1.03/ gallon
Aseptic drink boxes	7.95/ gallon

DEHYDRATED AND FREEZE-DRIED FOODS

DEHYDRATED	CANNED
Require small amount of shelf space	Require 3 to 4 times more shelf space
More expensive	More affordable
Extra water must be stored	Canning liquid can be used in other ways (soups, drinks, sauces, gravies, etc.)
More difficult to replace due to availability	Easily replaced
More to use up once the can is opened	More usable portions

Dehydrated and freeze-dried foods should be rotated every 3 to 5 years. Some have a shorter shelf-life and should be used regularly. These include milk and milk products, eggs and egg products, and margarine.

One pound of BUTTERMILK POWDER = 5 quarts liquid buttermilk
To use BUTTERMILK POWDER in baking, add the powder to dry ingredients and water with the liquid ingredients. 1 cup buttermilk = 1 cup water + 4 Tbsp. powder.

44 ounces MARGARINE POWDER = 5.5 pounds margarine
To mix MARGARINE POWDER, add 2 tsp. lukewarm water to 1 cup firmly packed margarine powder. Blend until creamy. Yield: 1/2 cup.

Use DRIED EGGS only in foods requiring thorough cooking.
One pound of DRIED EGGS = about 36 eggs
2-1/2 Tbsp. DRIED EGG + 2-1/2 Tbsp. water = 1 egg
To mix DRIED EGGS, place water in deep bowl. Sprinkle egg over surface and blend until smooth with a fork or rotary beater. Refrigerate. Use within a day.

EGG SUBSTITUTE -
FOR 1 EGG: Place 3 Tbsp. cold water in a small mixing bowl. Sprinkle 1 tsp. unflavored gelatin on the water to soften; beat. Add 2 Tbsp. + 1 tsp. boiling water and beat until dissolved. Place in the freezer to thicken, about 10 minutes. Take from freezer and beat until frothy with mixer. Add to batter in place of an egg. Use in baking only.
FOR 2 EGGS: 2 tsp. gelatin, 1/3 cup cold water, 1/3 cup boiling water. Prepare as for 1 egg.
FOR 3 EGGS: 1 Tbsp. gelatin, 1/2 cup cold water, 1/2 cup boiling water. Prepare as for 1 egg.

WHY HOME CAN?

1. Cost is less when fresh produce is in season or grown in home gardens.

2. Age of the canned good is known.

3. Some fruits and vegetables react with can linings after time - sometimes 9-12 months after purchase. Glass avoids this.

4. Salt and sugar content can be controlled.

5. Flavor is often better than commercially canned goods.

6. It teaches self-sufficiency.

7. It provides an opportunity to teach children work, self-sufficiency and cooperation.

CANNING QUESTIONS AND TIPS

Contact the County Extension Service for current canning information.

Review canning procedures each year to avoid forgetting an important step.

Check jar rims for cracks or chips.

Do not reuse sealing lids.

The size of fruits and vegetables makes a difference in the yield per pound. The less waste, the more jars of food produced. The amount of excess plant parts also follows the same rule. Don't pay for carrot tops, extra leaves and stems, etc. if you don't have to.

Fruits, tomatoes, pickles, jams and jellies may be canned in a water bath canner. Vegetables and meats MUST be canned in a pressure canner to insure a safe product.

To prevent fruit from darkening during preparation, drop it into water containing 2 tablespoons each of salt and vinegar per gallon. Drain just before heating or packing raw.

To insure that tomatoes are acidic enough to water bath can, add 1 teaspoon of lemon juice to each pint.

Always wipe jar rims before putting on hot lids.

Date jars before storing them.

CAN A PRESSURE SAUCEPAN BE USED FOR CANNING? If the pressure cooker has a gauge that maintains 10 pounds of pressure, it can be used for home canning.

WHICH PRESSURE CANNER IS MORE ACCURATE -- THE KIND WITH A DIAL OR THE ONE WITH A WEIGHT CONTROL? Both are accurate if used and cared for according to the manufacturer's instructions. Some people like numbers on a dial; others prefer the sight and sound of the weight control. Note: the dial control must be tested frequently for accuracy. (Check with the County Extension Service.) The weight control does not need this, but it must be cleaned occasionally for good service.

IS IT SAFE TO CAN WITHOUT SALT OR SUGAR? Salt and sugar are not necessary for safe processing of fruits and vegetables. The salt in recipes for pickle products and sugar in jams and jellies should not be reduced as the measures given are needed to provide good quality.

MAY I USE OLD MAYONNAISE JARS FOR CANNING? Yes, if you use them only for water bath canning for 30 minutes or less. Standard canning lids and rings will fit both wide-mouth and narrow-mouth mayonnaise jars.

FRUIT	POUNDS OF FRESH FRUIT PER QUART BOTTLED	IF YOU BUY CANNED FRUIT FOR …	IT'S THE SAME AS PAYING THIS MUCH PER POUND FRESH
Apples (sliced)	2-1/2 to 3 lb.	$1.49/20 oz.	$.78 - .99/lb.
(sauce)	2-1/2 to 3-1/2 lb.	1.99/50 oz.	.36 - .51/lb.
Apricots	2 to 2-1/2 lb.	1.13/16 oz.	.90 - 1.13/lb.
Berries, black	1-1/2 to 3 lb.	2.79/16 oz.	1.86 - 3.72/lb.
, blue	1-1/2 to 3 lb.	3.19/16 oz.	2.13 - 4.25/lb.
, goose	1-1/2 to 3 lb.	2.79/16 oz.	1.86 - 3.72/lb.
Cherries	2 to 2-1/2 lb.	1.57/16 oz.	1.27 - 1.57/lb.
Figs	1-1/2 to 2-1/2 lb.	2.39/16 oz.	1.91 - 3.19/lb.
Grapes	4 lb.	1.69/16 oz.	.85/lb.
Grapefruit	4 lb. (4 - 8 fruit)	1.39/16 oz.	.70/lb.
Loquats	3 to 4 lb.		
Nectarines	2 to 3 lb.		
Peaches	2 to 3 lb.	1.29/29 oz.	.48 - .71/lb.
Pears	2 to 3 lb.	1.29/29 oz.	.48 - .71/lb.
Plums	2 to 3 lb.	1.69/16 oz.	1.13 - 1.69/lb.
Rhubarb	1-1/3 to 2 lb.		
Tomatoes	2-1/2 to 4 lb.	.95/29 oz.	.26 - .41/lb

By knowing how much fresh fruit is needed to bottle one quart and how much commercially canned fruit costs, a judgment can be made as to whether it is cost effective to do home canning. For example, peaches would have to be less than $.71/lb and would have to be big enough to require only 2 pounds per quart before home canning could be less than the commercially canned product. Or, they would have to be less than $.48/lb if they are small and require 3 pounds per quart.

YIELD OF CANNED GOODS FROM
FRESH VEGETABLES

VEGETABLE	POUNDS OF FRESH VEGETABLES PER QUART BOTTLED	IF YOU BUY CANNED VEGETABLES FOR...	IT'S THE SAME AS PAYING THIS MUCH PER POUND FRESH
Asparagus (cut)	2-1/4 to 4-1/2 lb.	$1.15/10.5 oz.	$ .77 - 1.53
(whole)	2-1/4 to 4-1/2 lb.	2.29/15 oz.	.51 - 1.02
Beans, green	1-1/2 to 2-1/2 lb.	.43/16 oz.	.34 - .57/lb.
, lima	3 to 5 lb.	.69/17 oz.	.26 - .43/lb.
Beets	2 to 3-1/2 lb.	.44/16 oz.	.25 - .44/lb.
Carrots	2 to 3 lb.	.50/16 oz.	.33 - .50/lb.
Celery	1-1/2 to 2-1/2 lb.		
Corn	3 to 6 lb.	.44/16 oz.	.15 - .29/lb.
Mushrooms	1/3 to 1/2 lb./8 oz.	.79/4 oz.	3.16 - 4.65/lb.
Okra	1-1/2 lb.		
Peas	3 to 6 lb.	.44/16 oz.	.15 - .29/lb.
Potatoes, new	4 to 6 lb.	.50/16 oz.	.17 - .25/lb.
Pumpkin	1-1/2 to 3 lb.	.97/16 oz.	.65 - 1.29/lb.
Spinach (greens)	2 to 6 lb.	.50/16 oz.	.17 - .50/lb.
Squash, summer	2 to 4 lb.	.55/16 oz.	.28 - .55/lb.
, winter	1-1/2 to 3 lb.		
Sweet potatoes	2 to 3 lb.	1.09/29 oz.	.40 - .61/lb.
Turnips	2 to 3 lb.		

By knowing how many pounds of fresh vegetables are needed to bottle one quart and how much canned vegetables cost, a judgment can be made as to whether it is cost effective to do home canning. For example, mushrooms would be less expensive home canned than purchased if they could be purchased fresh for less than $3.16/lb. Carrots should be less than $.50/lb, and preferably less than $.33/lb, before they are home canned.

NON-FOOD BASICS

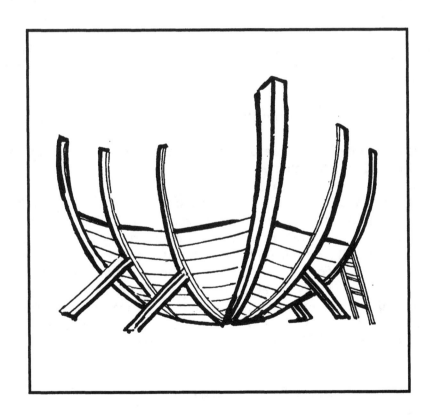

WATER STORAGE

Although it is difficult and impractical to store water in large quantities, experts recommend that a two-week emergency water supply be kept. Store at least fourteen gallons per person -- seven for drinking and seven for other uses. Store even more if there is a baby to care for.

When choosing a water storage container, remember that water weighs 8 pounds per gallon. Store water in thoroughly washed, clean containers, preferably of heavy plastic (not lightweight plastic that milk and water come in) with tight fitting caps. Plastic containers have the advantage of being shatterproof and lighter in weight than glass jugs or bottles. Five-gallon containers of rigid plastic are best for water storage. Glass jugs or bottles with screw tops are fine, but are heavier and break more easily. Metal containers tend to impart an unpleasant taste to the water after long storage. Bleach bottles are not appropriate for storing water for drinking or cooking, but are good for storing water for other uses. Water beds can be used for water storage for non-drinking purposes, but an algicide that is food-approved must be used.

Check containers every few months for leaks. At the same time check the water for cloudiness or undesirable appearance or taste. If undesirable appearances or tastes have developed, the water should be discarded.

When stored in clean containers, away from sunlight, and when free from bacteria at the time of storage, water will remain safe. Most disease organisms tend to die during long storage. Generally, the longer the water is stored, the safer it will become bacteriologically.

If the purity of water is in question, purify it with any of the following methods:

FILTRATION - Activated charcoal filters are best because they also remove some bad tastes. Some filters also add chemicals to kill bacteria.

CHEMICAL - All water purification chemicals should be rotated to ensure their activity.
1) Halazone tablets may be used according to package directions. 2) Iodine may be used in small amounts. Add three drops of 2% tincture of iodine to each quart of clear water, six drops for cloudy water. Stir thoroughly. 3) Household bleach that contains hypochlorite as its only active ingredient will purify water also. For clear water, add 2 drops per quart, 8 drops per gallon, or 1/2 teaspoon per 5 gallons. For cloudy water, add 4 drops per quart, 16 drops per gallon, or 1 teaspoon per 5 gallons. Stir and allow to stand 30 minutes. The water should have a chlorine odor. If it doesn't, add another dose and let stand 15 minutes. The smell of chlorine in the water is a sign of safety, so it is important NOT to use scented chlorine bleach.

BOILING - Boil water for 3-5 minutes. A higher elevation requires longer boiling to compensate for a lower boiling temperature. Add 1 minute for every 1,000 feet above sea level.

NON-FOOD STORAGE ITEMS

CLEANING
window cleaner
all-purpose cleaner
cleaning vinegar
baking soda
ammonia
floor cleaner
floor wax
furniture polish
furniture cleaner
cleanser
disinfectant
air freshener
toilet bowl cleaner
drain opener
dish soap
dishwasher soap
laundry detergent
fabric softener
pre-wash spray
bleach
oven cleaner
wood cleaner
insect spray
plunger
rags
mop
mop sponges
vacuum cleaner bags
brushes
bucket
clothespins
clothesline
sponges
dishcloths
SOS pads
scrub brush
pot scrubber
toilet brush
broom
dust pan

PERSONAL ITEMS
bath soap
lotion
powder
shampoo
toothbrushes
toothpaste
mouthwash
dental floss
deodorant
make-up
zinc oxide
shoe polish
razors
combs
brushes
feminine supplies
cotton swabs
cotton balls

MEDICATIONS
acetaminophen
ibuprofen
thermometer
cold medication
cough syrup
throat lozenges
cough drops
allergy medication
adhesive bandages
petroleum jelly
diarrhea medication
heating pad
ear drops
eye drops
nose drops
ipecac syrup
prescriptions taken regularly

PAPER GOODS
toilet paper
facial tissue
paper towels
napkins
foil
waxed paper
plastic wrap
plastic bags
paper bags
paper cups
paper plates
plastic silverware
moist towelettes

FUEL AND LIGHT
coal
oil
wood
charcoal
paper logs
sterno
propane
butane
white gas
kerosene
matches
candles
flashlight
batteries
flashlight bulbs
hurricane lamps
wicks
candle holders
light bulbs
lantern

EQUIPMENT
tools
wheat grinder
grain roller
bread mixer
canning equipment
dehydrator
sewing machine
radio
gardening equipment
portable toilet
coal or wood stove
grill or hibachi
sterno stove

MISCELLANEOUS
paper
pens
pencils
crayons
glue
envelopes
adhesive tape
shoe laces
rope
string
furnace filters
blankets
sleeping bags
cash
savings
how-to books

USES FOR VINEGAR

• Add cinnamon to some vinegar and microwave for a quick potpourri.

• Put on hands to remove fishy odors.

• Rub into deodorant stains in shirts before washing.

• Add a teaspoon to the water when cooking rice to make it fluffier.

• Add a teaspoon when cooking a beef roast to make it more tender.

• Make eardrops by mixing equal parts white vinegar and rubbing alcohol. Put 3-4 drops in each ear after swimming. The alcohol dries up the water and the vinegar kills the bacteria.

• When hand washing dishes, add vinegar to the rinse water for spot free glassware and china.

• To clean and polish stainless steel, chrome, ceramic and plastic, rub on full-strength vinegar, then polish dry with a cloth slightly dampened with water.

• Window cleaner - Mix 1/2 cup ammonia, 1/2 cup white vinegar, 2 tablespoons cornstarch in a bucket of warm water. Apply with a sponge and remove with a squeegee. If you don't have a squeegee, use black and white newsprint followed by dusting with a soft brush or duster.

• Drain cleaner - Pour 1/2 cup baking soda down the drain. Add 1 cup white vinegar and follow with boiling water. Flush with cold water for 1-2 minutes.

• General cleaner and disinfectant - 1 cup distilled white vinegar with 2 tablespoons lemon juice in 1-1/2 quarts of distilled water.

• Use cleaning vinegar (50% stronger than regular white vinegar) to remove tough hard water stains. Spray on, let sit briefly, and clean off with a scrubbing sponge.

To order Heloise's Versatile Vinegar Hints send $1.00 with a long, self-addressed, stamped envelope to:
    Heloise/Vinegar
    P.O. Box 19765
    Irvine, CA 92713

USES FOR BAKING SODA

TOOTH POWDER - Mix 1 Tbsp. salt and 5 Tbsp. baking soda. Add 6-9 drops of oil of peppermint or wintergreen and mix well. Label and keep in a tightly covered jar. To use, pour a small amount of powder into the palm of your hand, then wet toothbrush and rub bristles into the powder.

MOUTH WASH - Dissolve 2 tsp. salt and 2 tsp. baking soda in 1 quart of boiling water. Add 10 drops of oil of peppermint, wintergreen, or cloves. Label and keep in a covered jar. To use, rinse out mouth and gargle with small amount as often as desired.

ANTACID - 1/2 tsp. in glass of water every 2 hours up to maximum dosage, or as directed by a physician. (Do not take more than eight 1/2 tsp. for persons up to 60 years old or four 1/2 tsp. for persons 60 years or older in a 24-hr period, or use the maximum dosage of this product for more than 2 weeks.)

PLAY CLAY - Mix 2 cups baking soda with one cup cornstarch. Blend, and add 1-1/4 cups of cold water and mix until smooth. Boil one minute to consistency of moist mashed potatoes. Stir constantly. Spoon out onto a plate. Cover with damp cloth and cool. Knead lightly and roll out on waxed paper. Cut out designs with cookie cutter, bottle caps, or shape by hand. Etch in patterns. Let dry until hard (24-48 hours). Paint with tempera or water colors. Dry. Coat with clear shellac or clear nail polish. Mount pins, clips with white glue.

Baking soda may be used as a scouring powder, deodorizer, bath refresher and in many other ways.

Instructions for using baking soda for maintaining swimming pool chemistry are on the 4 lb. box.

For a free ARM & HAMMER Enviro-Use Wheel with other ways to use baking soda, send one 4 lb. box top, your name and address to:

ARM & HAMMER Enviro-Use Wheel Offer
P.O. Box 4533, Dept. P
Monticello, MN 55365-4533

For additional information write to:

Church & Dwight Co., Inc.
P.O. Box 7648E
Princeton, NJ 08543-7648

USES FOR PETROLEUM JELLY

• As a lipgloss

• To condition nails and cuticles, hands and feet

• To remove eye make-up

• To soothe minor burns and scrapes

• To help prevent diaper rash

• To help sticky drawers slide smoothly

• To remove water marks on wood furniture

• To clean marks off of shiny vinyl handbags and shoes

USES FOR SALT

• Discourage grass from growing between walkway bricks by sprinkling salt in the crevices.

• When oven spills occur, pour salt on them immediately. When cool, wipe up burned food more easily. This also works on spilled grease or an egg dropped on the kitchen floor.

• Salt, combined with lemon juice, removes brass tarnish; it also removes berry stains from hands.

• To prevent fruit from darkening during preparation for canning, drop it into water containing 2 tablespoons each of salt and vinegar per gallon of water. Drain just before heating or packing raw.

• Make nose drops for a stuffy nose by mixing 1/2 teaspoon salt with 1 cup water.

• Play Dough: 1 cup flour, 1 Tbsp oil, 1 cup water, 1/2 cup salt, 2 tsp cream of tartar. Stir in a heavy pan with a mixer. Color with food coloring. Stir until absolutely smooth. Cook on low heat until ball forms. While cooking, stir constantly. After ball forms, remove from stove and knead until consistency desired. When cool, store in an airtight container.

FUEL FACTS AND FIGURES

CANDLES: 3/4" diameter x 4" burns about 2 hrs. 20 min.
   7/8" diameter x 4" burns about 5 hrs.
   2" diameter x 9" burns about 7 hrs. per inch
   Store candles in a cool area. Store at least 3 candles per day.

CANNED HEAT: Stores easily and can be used indoors. A 7-ounce can burns about 1-1/2 hours. It will evaporate over long periods of time, especially if stored in a warm environment.

FLASHLIGHT: 2-battery with new batteries will run continuously for 6 hours. Store in a cool area. Many brands of batteries now have expiration dates on the package.

OIL: Emergency candles can be made from cooking oil. Take a piece of string, lay one end in cooking oil in a dish and allow the other end to hang over the edge. Light the dry end. Use 7 to 8 strings for more light. These are very smoky and should be used only when nothing else is available.

NEWSPAPER LOGS: Four logs burn approximately 1 hour and produce heat comparable to the same amount of wood on a pound-for-pound basis.

CHARCOAL: Use for outdoor cooking only. Store in metal containers to keep dry. When used in a foil oven, use 1 briquette for every 40 degrees of temperature desired. For Dutch oven cooking, use the oven size in inches plus 3 briquettes on top and the oven size in inches minus 3 briquettes on the bottom for 350 - 375°F heat.

KEROSENE: With a 1" wick, a kerosene lantern will burn for 45 hours on 1 quart. Burning 5 hours each day, the following amounts of kerosene would be used: Per day, 1/9 qt.; per month, 3-1/3 qts.; per year, 10 gallons. Kerosene is one of the least expensive liquid fuels. It stores for long periods and can be used indoors. To avoid the kerosene smell, start and extinguish lanterns outside.

WHITE GAS: To burn a 2 mantel lantern 5 hours a day, the following amounts of white gas would be used: Per day 5/12 qt.; per month, 3-1/8 gallons; per year, 38 gallons. For a two-burner stove burning 4 hours per day, the following amounts would be used: Per day, 1 qt.; per month, 7-1/2 gallons; per year, 91 gallons. White gas is the most costly and should be used outdoors.

PROPANE: Propane is very portable. It can be used indoors with good ventilation and is safe to store.

CAUTION*****DO NOT STORE LIQUID FUELS IN THE HOME OR WITHIN THE REACH OF CHILDREN.

FABRIC AND SEWING STORAGE

Store clothing or fabric for basic clothing items. Store in bins, plastic storage boxes, suitcases, cabinets, or plastic bags. To prevent color fading and mildewing, a cool, dark, dry storage place is necessary.

SEWING STORAGE LIST

fabric	snaps	safety pins
interfacing	gripper snaps	scissors
patterns	velcro	yarn
pattern paper	fasteners	embroidery floss
trims	zippers	bobbins
bias tape	buttons	machine oil
elastic	needles	machine light bulbs
thread	pins	machine needles

YARDAGE CONVERSION CHART*
Conversion figures are approximate

Fabric Width	35"-36"	44"-45"	52"-54"	58"-60"
	1-3/4	1-3/8	1-1/8	1
	2	1-5/8	1-3/8	1-1/4
Y	2-1/4	1-3/4	1-1/2	1-3/8
A	2-1/2	2-1/8	1-3/4	1-5/8
R	2-7/8	2-1/4	1-7/8	1-3/4
D	3-1/8	2-1/2	2	1-7/8
S	3-3/8	2-3/4	2-1/4	2
	3-3/4	2-7/8	2-3/8	2-1/4
	4-1/4	3-1/8	2-5/8	2-3/8
	4-1/2	3-3/8	2-3/4	2-5/8
	4-3/4	3-5/8	2-7/8	2-3/4
	5	3-7/8	3-1/8	2-7/8

For fabrics with a nap or one-way design, add at least 1/4 yard.
Adjust requirements accordingly for pattern alterations, large fabric designs, large pattern pieces, etc.

---

* Information source: Hancock Fabrics

FABRIC NEEDED FOR BASIC CLOTHING, IN YARDS
(45-inch Wide Fabric)

Items of Clothing	Infants	Children		Youth	Women			Men			Suitable Fabrics
		3-5 yrs	6-10 yrs	12-15 yrs	Small	Medium	Large	Small	Medium	Large	
Diapers (one dozen)	9										diaper flannel 27" wide
Receiving Blanket	2-1/2										print flannel 45" wide - Double
Sleep set	1-1/2										stretch knit, terry, brushed nylon
Dress (long-sleeves)	1/2	1	1-1/2	1-3/4 to 2	2-3/4	3	3-1/2				broadcloth, blends, polyester knits, prints
Petticoat	1/2	1/2	3/4	3/4	1	1	1				cotton, muslin, tricot
Underpants		1/4	1/4	1/2	1/2	1/2	1/2				cotton knit, tricot
Nightgown	1	1-1/2	1-3/4	3	3-3/4	4	4-1/4				flannel and tricot, brushed nylon
Coat	1	1-1/2	2-1/2	3	3-1/2	3-3/4	4	3	3-1/2	3-1/2	wool, double knits, corduroy
Shirt (long sleeves)		1-1/2	2	2-1/2	1-1/2	1-3/4	1-3/4	2	2-1/4	2-1/2	cotton and blends, flannel
T-shirt	1/2	1/2	3/4	1	1-1/4	1-1/2	1-3/4	1-1/2	2	2-1/4	knits, cotton, and blends
Robe (long)		1-1/2	1-3/4	3-1/8	2-3/4	3-1/8	3-1/4	4	4	4-1/2	terry, flannel, corduroy, quilted fabrics
Pajamas		1-3/4	2-3/4	3-1/4	3-1/2	3-1/2	4-1/2	4-1/4	4-1/4	4-3/4	flannel, cotton blends, prints
Pants-slacks	3/4	1	1-1/2	2	2-1/2	2-3/4	2-3/4	2-3/4	2-3/4	2-3/4	denim, polyester knits, corduroy, kettle cloth

From "Clothing and Fabric Storage," *Ensign*, July 1980, p. 61. Used by Permission.

ELECTRIC GRAIN MILLS

There are three kinds of electric grain mills: stone mills, burr plate mills and micronizing mills. Stone mills grind finer, produce less heat at finer settings, and wear better than steel burr plate mills. The steel burr plates are more versatile and some can grind not only grain but also shells, roots, bark, dried bones, spices, and animal feed. If the mill gets gummed up, the burr plates can be washed and then dried in an oven. Stones must never be washed.

With stones, you are limited to grinding dry materials of 12 percent moisture or less. Wet or oily materials, such as soybeans and peanuts, tend to coat the stones, making them useless. Stones can be cleaned by running through a handful of popcorn at a wide setting.

Micronizing mills produce a finer flour than even some stone mills. There is no glazing, overheating, or gumming because of the nature of the stainless steel milling heads. They will grind any grain and also beans.

When looking for a mill, look for low-heat, self-cleaning mills that produce a flour you would be happy making bread out of. Also consider ease of cleaning the outer parts of the mill, the size of the flour bin and the size of the mill itself.

HEAVY-DUTY MIXERS

Heavy-duty mixers vary in size, wattage, bowl size, and cost. Wattage varies from 235 watts to 1400 watts. In order to make 8 pounds of dough, which makes 4 large loaves of bread, a 6-quart bowl and at least 600 watts of power are needed. A 325 watt machine will handle it for a time but will eventually burn out.

When buying a machine, consider how much bread you will make how often. Also consider the bowl size, how easily ingredients can be added to the bowl, and ease of clean-up.

Most mixers of bread kneading capability also have other attachments. Sometimes, which attachments are available and their quality can help make a decision.

EMERGENCY PREPAREDNESS

EMERGENCY PREPAREDNESS
INFORMATION RESOURCES

AMERICAN RED CROSS OFFICE.

CITY OFFICE OF EMERGENCY MANAGEMENT.

EMERGENCY PREPAREDNESS HANDBOOK FOR MISSIONARIES. Barry and Lynette Crockett.

ESSENTIALS OF HOME PRODUCTION AND STORAGE. The Church of Jesus Christ of Latter-day Saints.

FAMILY EMERGENCY PLAN, VOL. 1. Barry and Lynette Crockett.

> Includes evacuation plans, 72-hr kits, sanitation, water, first aid kits, and what to do after a disaster.

FAMILY EMERGENCY PLAN, VOL. 2. Barry and Lynette Crockett.

> Includes earthquakes, volcanoes, landslides, fires, and power failures.

FAMILY EMERGENCY PLAN, VOL. 3. Barry and Lynette Crockett.

> Includes hurricanes, tornadoes, thunderstorms, floods, drought, and nuclear attack.

FAMILY HOME EVENING RESOURCE BOOK. The Church of Jesus Christ of Latter-day Saints.

NEWSPAPERS.

72-HOUR FAMILY EMERGENCY PREPAREDNESS CHECKLIST. Barry and Lynette Crockett.

SIMPLY PREPARED: A Guide to Emergency Preparedness and Food Storage. Cheryl Driggs. CFD Publications.

THE WEATHER CHANNEL. Customer service 1-800-364-4314. Education services 404-801-2503.

Check your local bookstore and library for additional titles.

Insurance companies and local utility companies usually offer free information concerning different aspects of emergency preparedness.

In areas of recurrent natural disasters, drug stores and grocery stores often have free information concerning disaster preparedness.

WEATHER TERMS

SEVERE THUNDERSTORM WATCH - Thunderstorms are expected in the area
SEVERE THUNDERSTORM WARNING - A thunderstorm is in the area which may produce high winds, hail, dangerous lightning, and/or tornadoes. Take cover immediately.

TORNADO WATCH - Weather conditions exist in which tornadoes may develop.
TORNADO WARNING - A tornado has been detected; take shelter immediately.

FLASH FLOOD WATCH - Flash floods are possible due to high rainfall amounts.
FLASH FLOOD WARNING - Flash flooding is occurring. Do not cross flooded areas.

TROPICAL DEPRESSION - Conditions similar to tropical storms but with winds less than 35 mph.
TROPICAL STORM - Similar to a hurricane but with winds ranging from 35 to 73 mph.

HURRICANE - A severe cyclonic storm, sometimes 500 miles across, with winds exceeding 74 mph.
CATEGORY 1 - 74-95 mph winds with a 4- to 5-foot storm surge.
CATEGORY 2 - 96-110 mph winds with a 6- to 8-foot storm surge.
CATEGORY 3 - 111-130 mph winds with a 9- to 12-foot storm surge.
CATEGORY 4 - 131-155 mph winds with a 13- to 18-foot storm surge.
CATEGORY 5 - 156 mph winds and above with a 19-foot storm surge and above.
STORM SURGE - An abnormally high tide caused by a hurricane. The cause of most deaths during a hurricane.
HURRICANE SEASON - The period of June 1 through November 30, during which hurricanes are most likely to develop.
HURRICANE WATCH - A hurricane is advancing and conditions are favorable for a hurricane to strike.
HURRICANE WARNING - A hurricane is expected to reach a coastal area within the next 24 hours.

HIGH WIND WARNING - Sustained winds of at least 40 mph lasting at least one hour are imminent.
GALE WARNING - Wind speed of 39-54 mph expected.

FREEZING RAIN OR DRIZZLE - Expected rain is likely to freeze as soon as it strikes the ground, putting a coating of ice or glaze on roads and all exposed surfaces.
ICE STORM - A substantial layer of ice is expected to accumulate from freezing rain.

HEAVY SNOW WARNING - A snowfall of four inches or more is expected in a 12-hour period, or a fall of six inches or more is expected in a 24-hour period. Variations of these rules may be used in different parts of the country depending on what the normal snowfall is.
BLIZZARD WARNING - Winds with speeds of at least 35 mph are accompanied by considerable falling or blowing snow. Temperatures of 20°F or lower are expected for an extended period of time.

HURRICANE SAFETY RULES

Prepare ahead!

CHECK emergency supplies before a hurricane threatens.

LEAVE low-lying areas before the hurricane strikes.

LEAVE mobile homes.

SECURE outdoor objects or bring them inside.

STORE drinking water in all available containers.

CHECK battery-powered equipment for fresh batteries.

KEEP your car fueled.

STAY at home, if your home is sturdy and on high ground.

REMAIN indoors.

BEWARE of the eye of the hurricane. Stay inside unless emergency repairs are absolutely necessary.

TORNADO SAFETY TIPS

TORNADO WATCH:
Tornadoes may develop

TORNADO WARNING:
Tornado detected; take shelter

IN HOMES--Stay away from windows and outside walls. Go to the basement or to an interior closet or small room. Get under something sturdy, if possible.

IN SCHOOLS OR FACTORIES--Move quickly (follow advance plans) to shelter areas or to an interior hallway on the lowest floor.

IN HIGH-RISE OFFICE BUILDINGS--Go to interior small rooms or hallways.

IN SHOPPING CENTERS--If available, go to designated shelter areas; otherwise, take cover in an interior rest room or small shop. Do not go to your car.

IN MOBILE HOMES--Damage can be diminished if the mobile home is properly blocked and anchored. Consult local or state authorities.

IN OPEN COUNTRY--Lie flat in the nearest depression with your hands shielding your head. Be alert for flash floods.

IN YOUR CAR--Do not try to outrun the tornado. If available, take shelter in a sturdy structure; otherwise, get out of your car and get into the nearest depression or ditch or into the "V" where an overpass meets the ground.

FLOOD SAFETY TIPS

• Make a home inventory list for insurance purposes.

• Learn the safest route from your home.

• Keep your car's gas tank one quarter to one half full.

• Have an emergency survival kit that includes copies of important documents.

• Be prepared to evacuate before water levels reach your property.

• If time permits and it is safe, turn off all utilities (in order: electricity, gas, water).

• If you get caught in your house, move to the second floor, or, if necessary, to the roof. Don't try to swim to safety.

• If outside, remember FLOODS ARE DECEPTIVE. Do not attempt to walk through water that is more than knee deep.

• Do not drive where water is over the roads.

• If your car stalls in flood waters, get out as soon as possible. One cubic yard of water weighs one metric ton.

FLOOD CLEAN-UP

CARPET - Use a wet/dry vacuum to pull out as much water as possible. Cut carpet on original seams. Pull it up and let it dry out. Discard the padding.

WOOD FLOORS - Pull up a few boards and use a wet/dry vacuum to pull out water underneath. Dry out the wood as soon a possible.

WALLBOARD - If dirty floodwaters soaked the wall board at least 4 feet above the floor, take down all the wall board and replace it. If the water was less than 4 feet deep, remove the lower 4 feet of wallboard.

WOOD FURNITURE - Put it up on boards or blocks and level it front to back and side to side. Clean with soap and water or oil soap. Furniture will dry in 4 to 6 weeks.

UPHOLSTERED FURNITURE - Unless furniture is antique or very valuable, it should probably be thrown out. Cleaning should be done only by a professional.

APPLIANCES - Most large appliances should be professionally cleaned. Consult an appliance repair service.

CAR - Cars that have water damage over the dash are usually considered a total loss. For carpets and seats, use a wet/dry vacuum and let the car air out. If the water was higher than the hubcaps, open the hood and let the electrical system dry out. Have the grease in the wheel bearings checked to see if it needs replacing.

LAWN TOOLS - Flush out the oil and gas tanks or take them to an authorized repair service.

CLOTHES - Hang clothes to dry as soon as possible. If clothes have picked up dye transfers, special treatment will be needed.

SHOES - Allow to air dry. Do not dry next to an oven or heater.

PAINTINGS - Move them into a room that is fairly dry. Bring the humidity level down to about 50%. Consult a specialist to determine if there is long-term damage.

BOOKS - Put books in an air-conditioned room in front of a dehumidifier. Do not use a hair dryer - it might burn the pages. At the same time, put dry pieces of paper between each page. Books may also need to be fumigated to kill mold spores.

POTTED PLANTS - Raise plants up on bricks to help drainage. Keep them in the shade until they come out of shock.

FOOD - Discard opened containers and packages of fresh meat, fish and poultry and unopened jars and bottles with paper seals. Do not use foods in canisters. Discard food in paper, cloth, cellophane, foil or cardboard. Throw away dented, bulging or leaking tin cans and jams and jellies sealed with paraffin. Discard all fruits and vegetables which do not have a natural peel, shell or coating which can be removed before use. Bottled carbonated beverages should be discarded if the caps are covered with silt.

Undamaged tin cans can be kept if the can is washed and sanitized before opening and the food is boiled before it is eaten. Fruits and vegetables should be washed in a strong detergent solution and scrubbed. Soak in a chlorine solution (1 Tbsp. bleach/ gallon water) for 15 to 20 minutes (this same solution will sanitize cans). Rinse with safe water, peel and cook thoroughly.

REFERENCES - Houston Chronicle June 28, 1989; "Emergency Food and Water" - Texas Agricultural Extension Service; REPAIRING YOUR FLOODED HOME - FEMA and the American Red Cross

CHEMICAL EMERGENCIES

Take action!

FIRST...
- Go indoors and listen to local radio or television for instructions.
- If you are in a vehicle, close windows and turn off and close air systems. Do <u>not</u> drive through a gas cloud.

SHELTER IN PLACE
- Close all windows and doors. Seal cracks with tape or cover with wet towels or blankets.
- Turn off heating, cooling or ventilation systems. Close fireplace dampers.
- Move to a central interior area of the building.
- Bring pets inside.
- If eyes, nose or throat become irritated, protect your breathing by covering your mouth with a damp cloth, take frequent shallow breaths, and stay calm.

IF EVACUATION IS ORDERED...
- Quickly gather essentials you and your family will need, such as medicine, baby supplies, driver's license, checkbook, and 72-hour kits.
- Do <u>not</u> go to children's schools. School officials will take special care of the children.
- Leave a sign on the door saying the house has been evacuated.
- Keep car windows and air vents closed.
- Police officers along the evacuation route will direct you.

EARTHQUAKE SAFETY TIPS

IN HOMES--Stay away from windows, hanging objects, fireplaces, and tall unsecured furniture. Get under a supported archway, against an inside wall, or under a heavy piece of furniture.

IN A HIGH-RISE BUILDING--Stay away from windows and glass partitions. Get under a heavy piece of furniture, against an inside corridor or hall, or near a pillar or support column.

IN A SHOPPING MALL--Move away from windows and display shelves. Move against an inside wall, corner, or doorway or get under a table, counter, or bench.

IN THE OPEN--Move away from buildings, if possible. To avoid flying glass, run to an open area or duck into a safe doorway. Stay away from waterways or swimming pools.

IN A CAR--Pull over and stop away from buildings, bridges, overpasses, underpasses, or overhead electrical wires. Keep your safety belt on.

FREEZING WEATHER PREPAREDNESS

Keep extra batteries for flashlights and radios and maintain an ample supply of food which requires no cooking or refrigeration in the event of power failures.

Be sure to have an adequate supply of warm clothing and bedding for each member of your family.

Use emergency cooking and heating facilities very carefully and only in well-ventilated areas.

In the event of a furnace failure, do the following to maintain minimum heat levels:
- Use an alternate heat source.
- Close off rooms which are not absolutely needed.
- Hang blankets over windows at night (let the sun shine in during the day). Stuff cracks around doors with rugs, newspapers, towels, or other such materials.

IN MILD CLIMATES:

Keep pipes from freezing. Wrap the pipes in insulation made especially for water pipes, or in layers of old newspaper, lapping the ends and securing them around the pipes. Cover the newspapers with plastic to keep out moisture. When it is extremely cold and there is real danger of freezing (temperatures below 32°F day and night for more than 24 hours), let the faucet that is furthest from the water inlet to the house drip a little. Although this wastes water, it may prevent freezing damage. Know where the valve for shutting off the water coming into the house or apartment is located. You may as a last resort have to shut off this main valve and drain all the pipes to keep them from freezing and bursting. If you have a sink against an exterior wall, leave the cabinet doors open beneath the sink to let in warm air during times of extreme cold. Also, shut off the water inlet valve to your sprinkler system and drain the system, if possible, to prevent broken pipes in the system.

If the pipes freeze despite efforts to prevent it, open faucets wide to allow for expansion of the frozen water. Remove any newspaper that may be around the pipe. Wrap pipes with rags and pour hot water over the rags, with the faucets still open.

Cover less hardy bushes and plants such as azaleas, camellias, and ferns when a hard freeze warning is issued.

Do not scalp lawns before winter. Leaving the grass a little long causes the roots to be longer. When roots are longer there is less chance of permanent damage or winter kill.

DISASTER RECOVERY

INSURANCE TIPS

TAKE photographs of the damage.

WAIT for an insurance adjuster before making permanent repairs.

MAKE only temporary emergency repairs.

KEEP receipts for repair materials.

BE THERE when the insurance adjuster comes.

IF YOUR FREEZER STOPS

Factors affecting how long food will stay frozen if you leave the freezer door shut are:
- **Amount of food in the freezer.** Food in a full freezer will stay frozen about two days; food in a freezer that is only half full may stay frozen up to one day. Keeping containers of ice in a partially filled freezer will help keep other foods in the freezer frozen longer.
- **Kind of food.** A freezer full of meat will not warm up as fast as a freezer full of baked goods.
- **Temperature in the freezer before it quit.** The colder the food, the longer it will stay frozen.
- **Amount of freezer insulation.** Obviously, a well-insulated freezer will keep food frozen much longer than one with little insulation.
- **Size of freezer.** The larger the freezer, the longer the food will stay frozen, particularly if the freezer is full.

If your freezer will be off longer than the 1 to 2 days the frozen food will remain frozen, you can extend that time by several methods.

--Wrap the freezer with crumpled newspapers and then blankets. Don't cover the air vents in case the freezer begins operating.

--Use dry ice to keep the temperature low. Place heavy cardboard over packages of frozen food; put the dry ice on top of the cardboard. Then keep your freezer closed. Be careful when using dry ice; wear gloves so that it won't burn your hands, and keep the room ventilated.

If food is safe to eat, it is safe to refreeze; if ice crystals remain in food, it is usually safe to refreeze it although there will be changes in the texture, flavor, and color and the nutritional value may be lower.

A common myth is that food must be cooked before it is refrozen. Frozen food will be of higher quality longer if it is not cooked (except for blanching vegetables). Cooked food can become unsafe faster if it is mishandled during thawing and preparation.

REFERENCE: Colorado State University Extension Service

EMERGENCY SANITATION

SEWAGE DISPOSAL

If you do not prepare ahead of time, a minor emergency could turn into a nightmare. Various conditions might arise that would prevent use of the bathroom. It is vital that some way be devised to dispose of human wastes. Failure to PROPERLY remedy the situation can lead to the rapid spread of bacteria and disease.

It is advisable to keep on hand some sanitation supplies, such as:

• A heavy plastic container with a tight fitting lid to use as an emergency toilet. This could be fitted with some kind of seat. An old toilet seat kept specifically for this purpose would be excellent.

• A larger container, also with a tight-fitting cover, to be used to empty the contents of the smaller container into for later disposal.

• Plastic bags to be used as liners. They would facilitate disposal of wastes and help to keep odors at a minimum.

• A supply of old newspapers and grocery sacks would be useful for wrapping garbage or lining waste containers.

• A reserve of toilet tissue, soap, and feminine hygiene items should be stored. Store 1 roll of toilet paper per person per week.

• A disinfectant such as chlorine bleach, lysol, or chlorinated lime.

Each time the temporary toilet is used, pour or sprinkle a disinfectant such as liquid chlorine bleach, lysol, or chlorinated lime into it. This will help keep down bacteria and odors.

Individual privacy is important. Screen temporary toilet facilities from view by hanging a blanket, sheet, canvas, or tarp.

If possible, bury the waste and accompanying garbage in a hole one to two feet deep. This depth is necessary to prevent dogs from digging it up, and to reduce the possibility of insects or rodents spreading bacteria and disease. The hole should be at least 50 feet away from a well, spring, or water supply and not in a flood prone area.

Be aware of the needs of an infant in the home, and store items such as diapers, extra blankets, and plastic pants.

Portable toilets may be purchased for about $50 to $125 and can provide 25 to 50 uses per tank depending on size. Many contain an automatic deodorizer and disinfectant.

GARBAGE AND TRASH DISPOSAL

Garbage sours and decomposes. It must be properly stored and handled if odor and insect problems are to be prevented. (Unless you already have a working compost pile.)

Wrap the garbage in several thicknesses of newspaper before putting it into your garbage containers. The paper will absorb some of the remaining moisture and make possible longer storage without unpleasant odors. A tight fitting lid on the garbage can is important to keep odors in, and flies and other insects out.

Garbage should be buried separately but in a like manner as body wastes.

Trash should be kept at a minimum and placed in a large container, separate from garbage. It can be burned or be kept until picked up by garbage services.

FIRST AID KITS

A good first aid kit should be serviceable every day as well as in disaster situations. A family first aid kit will be more practical if it is also a medicine chest. Storing all medicines and first aid supplies in one container allows them to be easily included on family trips and outings to provide for most medical and health needs. Store supplies in a closed container, preferably water resistant. Containers that work well are tool boxes, tackle boxes, and plastic storage containers. Keep the kit in a place where it can be used but not easily reached by young children.

Stock your first aid kit with items your family uses on a regular basis and those you may use in an emergency. Keep sufficient quantities for the size of your family but remember to rotate medications.

The following list is a guide:

antibiotic ointment	bandages, plastic strips
anti-fungal cream	ace bandages
anti-itch lotion	gauze pads (4" x 4")
prescription medications taken regularly	adhesive tape
pain relief tablets	bandages, sterile roll 2" & 4" wide
diarrhea medication	triangular bandage
laxative	sterile eye pads
eye drops	moist towelettes
ear drops (see page 48)	cotton balls
soap or antiseptic wash	cotton tipped swabs
nose drops (see page 50)	first aid manual
cough medicine	tweezers
allergy medicine	scissors
decongestant	single edge razor blade
motion sickness capsules or patches	needles and thread
throat lozenges	safety pins
antacid	water purification tablets
alcohol	plastic spoons
hydrogen peroxide	pocket knife
petroleum jelly	eye dropper
sunscreen lotion	thermometer
insect repellent	dental floss
syrup of Ipecac	paper cups or collapsible plastic cup
baking soda	space blanket
salt	safety matches
chemical cold pack	emergency phone numbers
chemical hot pack	phone money
sterile burn dressings	

72-HOUR EMERGENCY KIT
INSTALLMENT PLAN
(Quantities based on
2 people)

JANUARY

Acquire storage container/s - back packs, foot locker, suitcase, 5-gallon buckets, etc.

FEBRUARY

1. Flashlight (or 2 mini-flashlights) and batteries
2. 4 to 6 (8 ounce) boxes liquid milk
3. One change of clothing per person
4. Water purification tablets or bleach

MARCH

1. Trash bags (minimum 2)
2. 2 cans (about 5-7 ounces each) canned meat (tuna, chicken, ham, lunch meat, vienna sausage,
     OR equivalent in jerky and beef sticks)
3. 1 roll toilet paper
4. 2 pocket packages facial tissue

APRIL

1. 2 pounds crackers (crackers with peanut butter or cheese, graham crackers, pretzels, etc.)
2. Can opener
3. 2 gallons water
4. First aid kit

MAY

1. 1-1/2 to 2 pounds dried fruit
2. Bar of soap or bottle of liquid soap
3. 1/2 of emergency cash desired + phone money (coins)
4. List of emergency phone numbers/addresses

JUNE

1. 12 (8 ounce) boxes of juice
2. Radio and batteries
3. Emergency blanket
4. Scriptures

JULY

1. Hard candy and/or gum
2. Candles and waterproof matches
3. Bleach or other disinfectant
4. Consecrated oil

AUGUST

1. 18 ounce jar peanut butter
2. Sleeping bags or bed rolls
3. Hatchet
4. Plastic drop cloth or tarp

SEPTEMBER

1. 8 servings of fruit roll-ups, fun fruits or individual canned fruit
2. Stress release materials (coloring books, crayons, books, pen, pencil, paper, toys, games, etc.)
3. Remainder of emergency cash desired
4. Travel sewing kit

OCTOBER

1. Rope or cord
2. Baking soda
3. First-aid manual
4. Paper cups or 2 collapsible cups

NOVEMBER

1. Copy of legal documents
2. Wet wipes
3. Feminine needs
4. Towel and washcloth

DECEMBER

1. Plasticware
2. Infant needs
3. Specialized health needs
4. Paper towels

SAMPLE 72-HOUR FOOD KIT

6 (8 oz.) boxes juice
3 (8 oz.) boxes milk
2 granola bars
1/3 lb. graham crackers
5 (1.4 oz.) pkg. sandwich crackers
6 (.5 oz.) fruit roll-ups
4 (2 oz.) pkgs. trail mix
5 (1.5 oz.) pkgs. raisins
6 to 7-1/2 oz. peanut butter
3 ounce can tuna

7 beef jerky
1 package gum
fork
spoon
knife
18 wet wipes

Pack in an air and moisture-proof container

EMERGENCY MENU

DAY 1
1 milk
2 juice
1 granola bar
2 fruit roll-ups
1 pkg. trail mix
2 pkgs. raisins
3 oz. peanut butter
2 pkgs. sandwich crackers
3 jerky

DAY 3
1 milk
2 juice
2 fruit roll-ups
1 pkg. trail mix
2 pkgs. raisins
1/3 lb. graham crackers
1-1/2 oz. peanut butter
1 pkg. sandwich crackers
3 oz. can tuna
1 jerky

DAY 2
1 milk
2 juice
1 granola bar
2 fruit roll-ups
2 pkgs. trail mix
1 pkg. raisins
3 oz. peanut butter
2 pkgs. sandwich crackers
3 jerky

SAMPLE
THREE DAY EMERGENCY SUPPLY
FOR 6

FOOD per person

6 (8 oz.) boxes juice	6 to 7-1/2 oz. peanut butter
3 (8 oz.) boxes milk	3 ounce can tuna
2 granola bars	7 beef jerky
1/3 lb. graham crackers	1 package gum
5 (1.4 oz.) pkg. sandwich crackers	plastic fork
6 (.5 oz.) fruit roll-ups	plastic spoon
4 (2 oz.) pkgs. trail mix	plastic knife
5 (1.5 oz.) pkgs. raisins	18 individual wet wipes
food list and menu	

PAPER GOODS

Paper towels	1 roll
Paper sacks	2 large
Plastic bags	2 small, 1 large
Drop cloth	1
Facial tissues	6 pocket size

OTHER SUPPLIES

Hatchet	1
Ring saw	1
Pocket knife	1
Folding shovel	1
Candles	1
Citronella candle	1
Matches	4 boxes including waterproof and windproof
Batteries	2 9-volt
Flashlights	6
Lightsticks	6
Handwarmers	8
Lantern adaptor cord	1
Baking soda	1 small box
Soap	6 bottles
Clothes	3 XXL T-shirts, 3 XL T-shirts
Socks	6 pair
First aid kit	1
Pocket first aid kit	1
First aid manual	1
Topical antihistamine	1 tube
Mosquito repellant	1 bottle
Cash	$50
Water purification tablets	1 bottle
Rope	3-50 foot

Playing cards	1 deck
Paper	1 notebook
Activity books	1
Coloring books	2
Pencils	6
Colored pencils	1 small box
Emergency blankets	6
Plastic collapsible cups	6
Towel	1
Disinfectant spray	1 small can
Sewing kit	2 pocket kits
Toothbrushes with toothpaste	6
Combs	6
Dry shampoo	12 pouches
Feminine needs	assorted kinds and amounts
Rain ponchos	6
Business cards (for identification)	6
Phone numbers + phone money	6
Master supply list	2

TO GRAB
Sleeping bags
Document box
Water (1 gallon per person)
Portable toilet
Toilet supplies
Tent
Battery operated lantern
Weather radio
Large first aid kit

EXTRAS (if there is time!)
Cots
Camp stove
Tools
Books, magazines, games
Valuables
Scriptures

SAMPLE
EMERGENCY SURVIVAL PACKS
FOR 6

Each pack has:
  collapsible cup
  light stick
  pocket facial tissue
  travel toothbrush
  liquid soap
  dry shampoo
  comb
  hand warmer
  pencil
  mini flashlight
  grandparent's phone #
  telephone money
  Dad's business card
  rain poncho
  space blanket
  shirt
  socks
  3 milk boxes
  6 juice boxes
  2 food containers

Two food containers contain:
  2 granola bars
  1/3 lb. graham crackers
  5 pkg. sandwich crackers
  6 fruit roll-ups
  4 pkg. trail mix
  5 pkg. raisins
  6 to 7-1/2 oz. peanut butter
  3 oz. can tuna
  7 beef jerky
  1 pkg. gum
  fork
  spoon
  knife
  18 wet wipes
  menu

Packs for Dad and the oldest child are each a different color and different in color from the rest for easy identification.

Each pack has a card pinned to it. The card reminds the person, if there is time, to bring a sleeping bag, some water, and one or two of the following:

Battery-operated lantern
Toilet supplies
Weather radio
Portable toilet
Document box
Tent
Large first aid kit

If time allows, other items can be taken, such as:

Cots
Camp stove
Tools
Portable table
Books, magazines, games
Valuables

All lists, cards, and matches are in plastic resealable bags or containers.

Personal items are travel size, where possible.

In addition to the previous supplies, the packs also contain the following:

DAD

notebook
2 paper sacks
water purification tablets
matches
extra hand warmer
bug repellant
topical antihistamine

camp shovel
sewing kit
trash bags - 1 small, 1 large
hatchet
50 ft. rope
pocket knife
master list

OLDEST CHILD

50 ft. rope
plastic bag
2 9-volt batteries
pocket first aid kit

playing cards
cash
master list
pocket sewing kit

PACK #3

coloring book
first aid kit
50 ft. rope

towel
matches

PACK #4

colored pencils
coloring book
citronella candle
matches

paper towels
baking soda
lantern adapter cord

PACK #5

first aid manual
emergency candle
matches

feminine supplies
plastic ground cover
ring saw

PACK #6

extra hand warmer
puzzle book

feminine supplies
disinfectant spray

When putting together YOUR emergency survival packs, add what YOUR family needs. Consider age, gender, cost, and number of people to provide for. The kind of weather and natural disasters inherent to your area will also determine what you pack.

COLLEGE STUDENT
EMERGENCY PACK

collapsible cup
light stick
pocket facial tissue
travel toothbrush
liquid soap
dry shampoo
deodorant
comb
hand warmer
pencil
mini flashlight
grandparent's telephone number
phone money or a non-expiring phone card
Dad's business card (for identification)
rain poncho
space blanket
shirt
socks
cash in an envelope
pocket first aid kit
acetaminophen
playing cards
rope
feminine needs (for girls)
pocket sewing kit
water and wind proof matches
towel
notepaper
toilet paper (one roll flattened in a resealable
    bag)
camp trowel
pocket knife
9 aseptic water packs
3 milk boxes
6 juice boxes
2 food containers
list of pack contents

Two food containers contain:
  2 granola bars
  1/3 lb. graham crackers
  5 (1.4 oz.) pkg. sandwich crackers
  6 (.5 oz.) fruit roll-ups
  4 (2 oz.) pkg. trail mix
  5 (1.5 oz.) pkg. raisins
  6 to 7-1/2 oz. peanut butter
  3 oz. can tuna
  7 beef jerky
  1 pkg. gum
  fork
  spoon
  knife
  18 individual wet wipes
  food list and menu

(A 3600-calorie food bar may be substituted for
all of the food)

All lists, cards, and matches are in plastic
resealable bags or containers.

Personal items are travel size, where possible.

RECORD BASICS

DATE:

FINANCIAL INFORMATION

HUSBAND'S full name

   Social security number

   Husband's family's address and telephone

WIFE'S full name

   Social security number

   Wife's family's address and telephone

CHILDREN'S names and social security numbers

BANK

   Checking account number

   Savings account number

   Children's bank accounts

AGENT name, address, telephone number and account number for:

Health insurance

Life insurance
    Husband

    Wife

    Children

Disability insurance

Homeowner's insurance

Car insurance

Flood insurance

INVESTMENTS names and locations

PENSION plan

NAME, address, telephone number of people who owe us money

NAME, address, telephone number of people and companies we owe money

NAME, address, telephone number of:

Mortgage company

Lawyer

Accountant

Financial advisor

LOCATION of wills

SAFETY deposit box key location, location of box and list of contents

WHEN MOM'S GONE

PURPOSE: To provide information for the family or babysitter when Mom's gone in order to keep the household running as smoothly as possible.

Materials:
  1" binder or larger
  dividers
  plastic sheet protectors (if desired)
  plastic strips for putting magazines or booklets in binders (if desired)

COOKING
Include instructions for preparing foods that don't have a printed recipe easily found.

LAUNDRY
Include general laundry rules for sorting, washing, drying, and ironing. Some items may need specific instructions. If you have operating instructions for the washer and dryer, include them.

CLEANING
Include a cleaning schedule if you use one. List the children's normal chores. Other things to include could be: how much cleaner to use in mop water, how much water to give plants, garbage pick-up days, what temperatures to keep the air conditioner and furnace at.

DOCTORS
List names and phone numbers of doctors and dentists. Addresses could also be included.

SERVICES AND REPAIRS
List names and phone numbers of all service and repair people normally used including instrument tuners and repairman. Suggested: air conditioning/heating; cosmetic representative; electrician; hair salon; lawn care; pest control; piano tuner; plumber; roofer; spa/pool man; tree care; upholsterer; instrument shop; wallpaper hanger; brick layer; tile man; appliance repair
Include operating instruction manuals for appliances.

As you use it, you will find what you need to have or add. Individualize it for YOUR family.

BASICALLY FUN

PREPAREDNESS PARTY GAMES
INSTRUCTIONS

PREPARED TO GET TO KNOW YOU (page 85)

    Use this game as an icebreaker at the beginning of your party. It will help everyone to mingle and find out who is really prepared. If your group is large, limit everyone to using each person's name only once.

THE ID GAME (page 86)

    Prepare clear bags or other containers of each of the 22 beans. Label each with a letter. Using the provided list, see who can correctly identify all 22 kinds of beans.

    Prepare clear bags or other containers of each of the 20 grains and grain forms. Label each with a number. Using the provided list, see who can correctly identify all 20 grains and grain forms.

PREPARED TO GET TO KNOW YOU

Find someone who:

• Has a year's supply of basic food

• Has expanded food storage

• Has had a food storage Christmas

• Uses their wheat every month

• Has a grain mill

• Regularly uses powdered milk

• Had a garden this year

• Has a fruit tree

• Uses their food storage regularly

• Cans fruits and vegetables

• Dehydrates food

• Freezes fruits and vegetables

• Makes homemade bread

• Has made homemade cheese

• Knows how to sprout beans and grains

• Has made homemade yogurt

• Knows what quinoa is (and how to pronounce it!)

• Knows what triticale is

• Knows where anasazi beans come from

• Has done dry pack canning

• Has a good first aid kit

• Has a completed 72-hour kit

• Has water stored

• Has a fire escape plan

• Has a household inventory

• Has an emergency savings fund

• Has emergency heating supplies

• Has emergency light sources

• Has had CPR training

THE ID GAME

BEANS

Lentils	Great Northern	Red	Small White
Split peas	Garbanzo	Whole peas	Pigeon peas
Kidney	Baby Lima	Yellow peas	Large Lima
Pinto	Blackeye peas	Adzuki	Red lentils
Black	Soybeans	Anasazi	Navy
Pink	Fava		

A.	G.	M.	S.
B.	H.	N.	T.
C.	I.	O.	U.
D.	J.	P.	V.
E.	K.	Q.	
F.	L.	R.	

GRAINS

Barley	Oat Groats	Buckwheat	Quinoa
Wheat	Oatmeal	Millet	Amaranth
Brown Rice	Corn	Popcorn	Teff
White Rice	Cornmeal	Bulgur	Kamut
Wild Rice	Rye	Grits	Spelt

1.	6.	11.	16.
2.	7.	12.	17.
3.	8.	13.	18.
4.	9.	14.	19.
5.	10.	15.	20.

INSTRUCTIONS FOR
PREPARING AND PLAYING
"FAMILY PREPAREDNESS FUN"

PREPARATION

Mount pages, or copies of pages, of playing cards and answer sheets on light-weight cardboard or tag board OR cover with laminating plastic. Cut pages of cards into individual cards.

RULES OF PLAY

Form teams or play as individuals.

Mix up the cards and place them in one stack face down.

An individual draws one card, reads it aloud and answers it. Answers can be found by number on the answer sheets. Correct answers receive 5 points. The turn continues until a question is answered incorrectly or until three questions have been answered correctly, whichever comes first. Play then continues in a clockwise direction.

Some questions have bonus questions which may be attempted when a question is answered correctly. If the bonus question is answered incorrectly, the player may still continue with the next card. Bonus questions answered correctly give the team or player an additional 5 points.

Blessing cards give the team or player 5 points without having to answer a question.

The first team or player to reach a pre-determined number of points is the winner.

#1 A thunderstorm knocked out the power. You forgot to buy new batteries for your flashlight. Skip 1 turn.	**#5** How many days worth of food should you have in your 72-hour kits?
#2 Which term indicates that a particular weather phenomenon is occurring - watch or warning?	**#6** How many months' salary should you save to have a year's supply of money?

#3
 	
If you are in your car and spot a tornado coming toward you, what should you do?
  a) try to outrun it in your car
  b) get out and run
  c) get out and get in a ditch or ground depression
	#7
	
	What are four of the six areas of Personal and Family Preparedness?

#4
 	
If you are at home or work and a tornado warning is issued, what should you do?
  a) run outside
  b) go to an interior hall or closet
  c) ignore the warning
	#8
	
	How many pounds of grains and grain products are recommended for a year's supply for one person?
	
	BONUS: How much of it should be whole grains?

#9 How many pounds of powdered milk per person is recommended for storage? BONUS: When can it be less?	**#13** Your fruit trees produced so well that you had enough to can and to share. You are blessed with another turn.
#10 What is the minimum amount of gasoline to keep in your car to be prepared for emergencies?	**#14** You have been faithful about having Family Home Evening. You are blessed with another turn.
#11 You use your food storage regularly. You are blessed with another turn.	**#15** Where should at least 1 copy of your household inventory be stored?
#12 You planted a garden and kept it weeded. You are blessed with another turn.	**#16** Name 2 ways to purify water.

#17	#21
Name 2 emergency light sources.	In what order do you turn off utilities?

#18	#22
Name 2 emergency cooking methods.	For having home and medical insurance, you are blessed. Take one free turn.

#19	#23
Name 2 emergency heat sources.	Name one prophet in the Old Testament whose preparedness saved his family.

#20	#24
When you have both a refrigerator/freezer and a deep freezer, in what order do you use refrigerated and frozen foods when the power goes out?	Cite one instance in the Book of Mormon when the people were prepared to live without yearly crops for an extended period of time.

#25	#29
COMPLETE: Wherefore, verily I say unto you that all things unto me are _____, and not at any time have I given unto you a law which was _____ ... (D&C 29:34)	COMPLETE: But if any provide not for his ___, and specially for those of his own ____, he hath _____ the faith, and is worse than an _____. (I Timothy 5:8)
#26	#30
COMPLETE: Preparedness, when properly pursued, is _ __ _ ___, not a sudden spectacular program. --Spencer W. Kimball	COMPLETE: ... if ye are _____ ye shall not ____. (D&C 38:30)
#27	#31
COMPLETE: Let every head of every household see to it that he has on hand enough ____ and _____, and, where possible, ____ also, for at least a ____ ahead. --J. Rueben Clark BONUS: In what year did Pres. Clark make this statement?	COMPLETE: ... do ye suppose that the Lord will still _____ us, while we sit upon our thrones and do not ____ ___ of the means which the Lord has _____ for us? (Alma 60:21)
#28	#32
COMPLETE: The revelation to store food may be as essential to our temporal salvation today as _____ the ___ was to the people in the days of ____. --Ezra Taft Benson	Name 4 conditions which might require you to use your food storage.

#33 TRUE or FALSE A month's supply of basic foods for 1 adult can be purchased for less than $20.	#37 Name 2 reasons why the basic foods should be stored first.
#34 Name 4 different grains.	#38 What is basic storage?
#35 Name 4 different beans.	#39 What is expanded storage?
#36 Name 2 family activities that would promote preparedness and self-reliance.	#40 TRUE or FALSE High temperatures have no effect on the shelf life of food.

#41	#45
What are the 4 key words to storage conditions?	When is it necessary to store vitamins?

#42	#46
What is "shelf life"?	Is one pound of dry beans equal to one pound of cooked beans? BONUS: If "no", what is it equal to?

#43	#47
Why should foods be "dated"?	Name 4 fruits and/or vegetables that should be among the first added to basic storage. BONUS: Why are they first?

#44	#48
TRUE or FALSE Seeds may be stored for future planting and they will still sprout properly.	COMPLETE: Eat what you _____ and _____ what you ___.

#49 Name 3 ways to afford home storage.	**#53** What is one effect light has on food?
#50 TRUE or FALSE It is all right to go into debt to purchase food storage.	**#54** TRUE or FALSE Plastic trash bags should always be used to line storage buckets.
#51 What is the maximum moisture content for most dry foods to store well? a) 5% b) 10% c) 15%	**#55** What is the most important characteristic of a good storage container?
#52 Weevil cannot grow in grain with less than how much moisture? a) 10% b) 15% c) 18%	**#56** What is the most important step to remember when treating storage foods with dry ice? BONUS: What will happen if you don't?

#57 The only way to can vegetables and meats is by what method?	**#61** TRUE or FALSE Do not mix old and new beans or they will cook unevenly.
#58 The best way to can fruit, jams, jellies, and pickles is by what method?	**#62** Which has more calories per tablespoon - honey or sugar?
#59 Name a way to test old wheat for acceptable protein value.	**#63** TRUE or FALSE Honey that crystallizes is better for storage than honey that remains liquid. BONUS: Why?
#60 TRUE or FALSE Gluten is an excellent meat substitute.	**#64** TRUE or FALSE At least half of the salt stored should be iodized.

#65

TRUE or FALSE
Dehydrated and freeze-dried foods never have to be rotated.

#69

TRUE or FALSE
Included in emergency preparedness is being able to contact emergency personnel, having a fire extinguisher and having an emergency evacuation plan.

#66

TRUE or FALSE
The longer water is stored, the safer it will be bacteriologically, if the water and container were clean originally.

#70

A tropical storm becomes a hurricane when the winds reach
a) 56 mph
b) 74 mph
c) 81 mph

#67

How many gallons of water should be stored for each person for 2 weeks?

#71

COMPLETE: Hurricane season is (month) 1st through (month) 30th.

#68

TRUE or FALSE
When considering a grain mill, it is preferable to find a low heat producing mill.

#72

If flooding threatens your home, should you evacuate before or after it floods?

#73 TRUE or FALSE If your car stalls in high water, it is safe to stay in the car.	**#77** Which fuel is the most expensive?
#74 TRUE or FALSE Undamaged tin cans that have been in flood waters are safe to use without any special treatment.	**#78** TRUE or FALSE If food is safe to eat, it is safe to refreeze.
#75 How long can the outside temperature be below 32 degrees before unprotected pipes will begin to freeze? a) 18 hours b) 24 hours c) 30 hours	**#79** TRUE or FALSE You should <u>always</u> evacuate if a hurricane warning is issued for your area.
#76 Name a fuel which is safe to use indoors with good ventilation.	**#80** If a freezer is without power and is kept closed, the food will stay good for an average of: a) 12 hours b) 36 hours c) 48 hours

#81 COMPLETE: And why call ye me, ___, ___ and do ___ the things which I say? (Luke 6:46)	#85 In an emergency situation, how should waste and garbage be disposed of?

#82
 	
If you are indoors when an earthquake strikes, you should
  a) run outside
  b) stay there and go to a safe location in that room
  c) sit down in the middle of the floor
	#86
	
	For practicing your family fire drill at least annually, you are blessed with another turn.

#83
 	
If you are outside when an earthquake strikes, you should
  a) run inside
  b) crawl under a car
  c) move away from tall structures into an open space
	#87
	
	Name 2 existing places in a home that food can be stored.

#84 Name one area of a room where you should take refuge from an earthquake.	#88 TRUE or FALSE It is better to have one month's supply of food than to have none at all.

ANSWERS TO
"FAMILY PREPAREDNESS FUN"

1. Skip 1 turn

2. Warning

3. C

4. B

5. 3 days

6. 3 to 4 months

7. Home storage
   Social, emotional, and
    spiritual strength
   Health
   Resource management
   Employment
   Education

8. 300 lbs.; 2/3

9. 75 lbs.; when more grains are stored and used

10. 1/4 tank

11. Blessing

12. Blessing

13. Blessing

14. Blessing

15. Away from home

16. Filtration; purification tablets; iodine; chlorine bleach; boiling

17. Flashlight; candle; oil lamp; battery lantern; kerosene lantern; light stick

18. Charcoal; gas grill; fireplace; sterno; gas stove; "buddy" burner; hibachi

19. Fireplace; gas heaters; hot hands

20. 1-Refrigerator, 2-refrigerator freezer, 3-deep freezer

21. 1-Electricity, 2-gas, 3-water

22. Blessing

23. Noah; Joseph of Egypt

24. Nephi's people in Helaman chapter 11; Nephites at war with the Gadianton robbers in 3 Nephi chapter 4.

25. spiritual; temporal

26. a way of life

27. food; clothing; fuel; year

28. boarding; ark; Noah

29. own; household; denied; infidel

30. prepared; fear

31. deliver; make use; provided

32. Trucking strikes
    Natural disasters
    Recession
    Depression
    Crop failure
    Drought
    Unemployment
    Disability
    Unforseen expenses
    Death of breadwinner
    War

33. True

34. Wheat; rice; oats; barley; rye; buckwheat; millet; amaranth; teff; quinoa; corn; Job's tears; milo; spelt; triticale; kamut

35. Kidney; great northern; small white; pinto; lima; pink; black; navy; lentils; whole and split peas; soybeans; adzuki; anasazi; blackeye; red; Roman; garbanzo; fava; pigeon

36. Emergency drills; utility shut off; put together emergency kits; rotate emergency supplies; basic sewing; basic cooking; use of tools; basic home repairs; financial management; exercise; gardening; directing music; etiquette; ideas in the Family Home Evening resource manual; playing this game

37. Long shelf life; least expensive; most nutrition for the volume; provide all nutrients including some Vit A and Vit C; basis of a healthy disease prevention diet.

38. Life sustaining foods that store well - grains, legumes, fats, sugars, salt, milk

39. Foods beyond basic storage

40. False

41. Cool, dry, dark, airtight

42. The point at which a food begins to deteriorate

43. To know how old they are

44. True

45. When fruits and vegetables are not stored.

46. No
It is equal to 2 pounds of cooked or canned.

47. Tomatoes; spinach; greens; yams; carrots; apricots; pumpkin; mixed vegetables; peas; squash; peaches; sweet potatoes; oranges; corn; peppers
They are good sources of Vit A and Vit C.

48. store; store; eat

49. budget; income tax return; bonuses; Christmas; garden; trim food budget; checking account interest; stock up on sales; cut recreation by 50%; forgo a vacation; cut clothing budget down; sell luxury possessions; buy in bulk

50. False

51. B

52. A

53. Fades color; destroys vitamins; speeds rancidity

54. False

55. Being airtight

56. Wait for the dry ice to completely sublimate before sealing the lid down; the lid will blow off.

57. Pressure canning

58. Water bath canning

59. Sprout to see if at least 50% will sprout; Bake bread out of the flour to see if acceptable bread can be made.

60. False

61. True

62. Honey has 65 cal/Tbsp. while sugar has 45 cal/Tbsp.

63. True.
Honey that will crystallize will not support growth of spoilage organisms and helps prevent fermentation.

64. True

65. False

66. True

67. 14 gallons

68. True

69. True

70. B

71. June; November

72. Before

73. False

74. False

75. B

76. Kerosene; propane; canned heat

77. White gas

78. True

79. False

80. B

81. Lord, Lord; not

82. B

83. C

84. Under a supported archway; against an inside wall; under a heavy piece of furniture

85. It should be buried 1-2 feet deep.

86. Blessing

87. Under beds, in closets, in cabinets, behind furniture, as part of furniture

88. True

The following were sources of information for some of my handouts. Some of the material used has been passed from class to class without a source being known. Others come from experience. Thank you to all of them.

CANNING, FREEZING, AND DRYING. Editors of Sunset Books and Sunset Magazine. Lane Publishing Company.

Colorado State University Extension Service.

THE COMPLETE WHOLE GRAIN COOKBOOK. Carol Gelles. Donald I. Fine, Inc.

Dr. Hal Johnson, BYU Department of Food Science and Nutrition

EMERGENCY PREPAREDNESS HANDBOOK FOR MISSIONARIES. Barry and Lynette Crockett.

THE ENCYCLOPEDIA OF COUNTRY LIVING. Carla Emery. Sasquatch Books.

ESSENTIALS OF HOME PRODUCTION AND STORAGE. The Church of Jesus Christ of Latter-day Saints.

FAMILY EMERGENCY PLAN, VOL. 3. Barry and Lynette Crockett.

GRAINS. Joanne Lamb Hayes and Bonnie Tandy Leblang. Harmony Books.

HOUSTON CHRONICLE.

HOME CANNING OF FRUITS AND VEGETABLES. USDA Bulletin No. 8.

HOME FOOD SYSTEMS. Rodger B. Yepsen, Jr., Editor. Rodale Press.

JUST IN CASE. Barbara Salsbury. Bookcraft Publishers.

MAKING THE BEST OF BASICS: Family Preparedness Handbook. James Talmage Stevens. Gold Leaf Press.

THE NEW LAUREL'S KITCHEN. Laurel Robertson, Carol Flinders, and Brian Ruppenthal. Ten Speed Press.

REPAIRING YOUR FLOODED HOME. FEMA and the American Red Cross.

SOUTHERN LIVING MAGAZINE.

Texas Agricultural Extension Service.

THE TIGHTWAD GAZETTE. Amy Dacyczyn. Villard Books.

TUFTS UNIVERSITY DIET AND NUTRITION LETTER.

Order Form

To order additional copies of *Simply Prepared,* make a copy of this form, send your name, address, and $12.95 + shipping for each copy ordered to:

Cheryl Driggs
6727 Saffron Hills
Spring, Texas 77379

NAME: _____

ADDRESS: _____

_____

NUMBER OF COPIES OF *SIMPLY PREPARED:*_____

AMOUNT ENCLOSED: _____

Shipping: For 1 or 2 books, add $2.00 per book.
                 For 3 or more books, add $1.00 per book.

Please make checks payable to Cheryl Driggs.
Be sure to write any special delivery instructions or requests on this form.

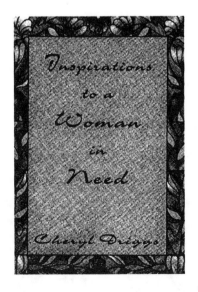

If you would like a copy of Cheryl's book,
Inspirations to a Woman in Need,
please send $6.00 + shipping for each copy ordered.
(If ordered with *Simply Prepared*, shipping of
Inspirations to a Woman in Need is free)

Please send me _____ copy(ies) of
Inspirations to a Woman in Need, by Cheryl Driggs.